CW00481680

Cartimandua
QUEEN OF THE BRIGANTES

.

Cartimandua
QUEEN OF THE BRIGANTES

NICKI HOWARTH

For Bill and Marie, my parents, for their encouragement and support. For Veronica, whose teaching made the past seem so alive and vivid, and especially for David, who made the realisation of a dream possible.

First published 2008

The History Press Ltd
The Mill, Brimscombe Port
Stroud, Gloucestershire, GL5 2QG
www.thehistorypress.co.uk

© Nicki Howarth, 2008

The right of Nicki Howarth to be identified as the Author
of this work has been asserted in accordance with the
Copyrights, Designs and Patents Act 1988.

All rights reserved. No part of this book may be reprinted
or reproduced or utilised in any form or by any electronic,
mechanical or other means, now known or hereafter invented,
including photocopying and recording, or in any information
storage or retrieval system, without the permission in writing
from the Publishers.
British Library Cataloguing in Publication Data.
A catalogue record for this book is available from the British Library.

ISBN 978 0 7524 4705 6

Printed in Great Britain

Contents

List of Figures

CHAPTER FRONTISPIECES

Acknowledgements

This book could not have been written without the generosity and patience of a number of individuals. My mind is a museum and these permanent 'exhibits' were chosen after consulting people with knowledge far beyond my own. My particular thanks go to Simon James, David Braund, John Creighton, William Hanson, Neil Faulkner, Percival Turnbull, Lindsay Allason-Jones and Ian Leins, who all listened to my inane questions and politely answered them in great detail. In particular, Colin Haselgrove and Katherine Bearcock were kind enough to spare their time on a one-to-one basis and I am extremely grateful for their help and interest in the project. Any errors or mistakes in the book are entirely my responsibility and without the help of the people mentioned above, there would no doubt be many more of them. I must thank Philip de Jersey and the Institute of Archaeology, University of Oxford, for allowing me to use their image of the Volisios-Cartivellaunos gold stater from the Celtic Coin Index (www.finds.org.uk/CCI), and Dryad Designs very kindly allowed me to include their 'Cernunnos' design in the book.

The beautiful original artwork was contributed by the talented artist David Pollard (www.davidgpollard.com). With his attention to detail, genuine interest in the subject matter and immense creativity he was a pleasure to work with.

I would like to express my gratitude to my editors, Peter Kemmis Betty and Wendy Logue, for giving me the opportunity to explore this idea and the flexibility to finish the piece.

The cover photograph was reproduced with the kind permission of York Museums Trust (Yorkshire Museum), figure 5 with the kind permission of SCRAN and The National Museums Scotland, and figure 9 with the kind permission of the British Museum.

Note on Translations Used

Appian – *The Civil Wars* (Loeb Classical Library, 1913). Available at: http://penelope.uchicago.edu/Thayer/E/Roman/Texts/Appian/Civil_Wars/1★.html#116 (Accessed 9 January 2008)

Cassius Dio – *Roman History* (Loeb Classical Library edition, 1917). Available at: http://penelope.uchicago.edu/Thayer/E/Roman/Texts/Cassius_Dio/53★.html (Accessed 30 November 2007)

Cormac, king of Cashel – *Cormac's Glossary* (translated by Whitley Stokes 1862, London: Williams and Norgate). Available at: www.openlibrary.org/details/threeirishglossaoocormuoft (Accessed 7 December 2007)

Geoffrey of Monmouth – *History of the Kings of Britain* (translated by Aaron Thompson, revised by J.A. Giles 1999). Available at: www.yorku.ca/inpar/geoffrey_thompson.pdf (Accessed 31 January 2008)

Herodotus – *The Histories* (translated by A.D. Godley). Available at: www.perseus.tufts.edu/cgi-bin/ptext?lookup=Hdt.+2.100.1 (Accessed 28 January 2008)

Josephus – *The Antiquities of the Jews* (translated by William Whiston). Available at: http://en.wikisource.org/wiki/The_Antiquities_of_the_Jews/Book_XX#Chapter_7 (Accessed 27 January 2008)

Julius Caesar – *Gallic War* (translated by W.A. McDevitte and W.S. Bohn 1869). Available at: www.perseus.tufts.edu/cgi-bin/ptext?lookup=Caes.+Gal.+6.21 (Accessed 11 December 2007)

Juvenal – *Satires* (translated by G.G. Ramsay). Available at: www.fordham. edu/halsall/ancient/juvenal-satvi.html (Accessed 17 January 2008)

Livy – *The History of Rome* (translated by Rev. Canon Roberts 1905). Available at: http://mcadams.posc.mu.edu/txt/ah/Livy/Livy34.html (Accessed 2 January 2008)

Pliny the Elder – *The Natural History* (translated by John Bostock and H.T. Riley 1855). Available at: www.perseus.tufts.edu/cgi-bin/ptext?lookup=Plin. +Nat.+30.4 (Accessed 4 January 2008)

Plutarch – *The Parallel Lives* (Loeb Classical Library edition 1920). Available at: http://penelope.uchicago.edu/Thayer/E/Roman/Texts/Plutarch/ Lives/Antony*.html (Accessed 30 January 2008)

Ptolemy – *The Geography* (translated by Edward Luther Stevenson 1932). Available at: http://penelope.uchicago.edu/Thayer/E/Gazetteer/ Periods/Roman/_Texts/Ptolemy/home.html (Accessed 6 December 2007)

Seneca – *Apocolocyntosis* (translated by W.H.D. Rouse 1920). Available at: www.gutenberg.org/files/10001/10001-h/10001-h.htm (Accessed 6 December 2007)

Statius – *The Silvae* (translated by D.A. Slater 1908). Available at: www. elfinspell.com/Statius/SilvaeBk5Letter2.html (Accessed 22 January 2008)

Strabo – *Geography* (eds H.C. Hamilton and W. Falconer 1903). Available at: www.perseus.tufts.edu/cgi-bin/ptext?lookup=Strab.+4.5.1 (Accessed 30 November 2007)

Suetonius – *The Twelve Caesars* (translated by Robert Graves and revised by Michael Grant 1989)

Tacitus – *The Agricola and The Germania* (translated by H. Mattingley and revised by S.A. Handford 1970)

Tacitus – *The Annals of Imperial Rome* (translated by M. Grant 1996)

Tacitus – *The Annals of Imperial Rome* (translated by Alfred John Church and William Jackson Brodribb 1942). Available at: www.perseus.tufts.edu/cgi-bin/ptext?doc=Perseus:text:1999.02.0078:book=12:chapter=40 (Accessed 2 January 2008)

Tacitus – *The Histories* (translated by Kenneth Wellesley 1995)

Tacitus – *The Histories* (translated by W.H. Fyfe, revised and edited by D.S. Levene 1997)

Tacitus – *The Histories* (translated by Alfred John Church and William Jackson Brodribb 1942). Available at: www.perseus.tufts.edu/cgi-bin/ptext?doc=Perseus:text:1999.02.0080:book=3:chapter=45 (Accessed 2 January 2008)

Vegetius – *The Military Institutions of the Romans* (translated by John Clarke 1767). Available at: www.pvv.ntnu.no/~madsb/home/war/vegetius/dere05.php#01 (Accessed 31 January 2008)

ABBREVIATIONS

RIB   Collingwood, R.G. and Wright, R.P. (1965), *The Roman Inscriptions of Britain, vol.1: Inscriptions on Stone*, Oxford: Oxford University Press. Available at: http://www.roman-britain.org/epigraphy/rib_index.htm (Accessed 10 December 2007)

CCI   Celtic Coin Index. Available at: www.finds.org.uk/CCI/ (Accessed 29 December 2007)

Preface

There was no label this time with the words 'DRINK ME', but nevertheless she uncorked it and put it to her lips. 'I know *something* interesting is sure to happen,' she said to herself, 'whenever I eat or drink anything; so I'll just see what this bottle does.

Lewis Carroll, *Alice in Wonderland*

Looking back through time is like going down the rabbit-hole – much like Alice, we have to change ourselves and our perceptions to fit into this new world. Seeing the reality of the past as its inhabitants would have done is impossible – we have our own beliefs, biases and baggage. In many cases, there are no answers to the multitude of questions: only educated guesses, best estimates and the testimony, if we are lucky, of individuals with their own agendas. Investigating a society with no written history, a mainly oral tradition and the only contemporary reports coming from a 'conquering race' means that the problem of uncovering the past with any certainty is compounded, but does this mean that we should not try?

There is no such thing as an impartial observer. As with forensics, where we change any matter that we come into contact with, our own personal biases affect our judgement however much we try to remain objective. Age, sex, education, upbringing, generational values and a wealth of experience will all shape the way we process and understand information. That said, I have attempted to draw on all the resources at my disposal – I have read the academic journals, books and papers, and the popular volumes, for I believe that inspiration and often the answer to any vexing question may sometimes be presented from the most unlikely direction.

I often reference popular media in my initial attempts to digest and assimilate information. The first time I remember hearing about Cartimandua, she struck me as the Alexis Carrington of many a history book. These scholarly texts portrayed her as the 'power-hungry seductress', whilst Boudica alternated between the 'wronged mother' and 'vengeful harpy' stereotypes. Other, feminist, literature attempted to redress the balance, as the classical writers seem somewhat chauvinistic by modern-day standards. These two extremes went from black straight across to white on the colour spectrum. My palette is less monotone – hopefully shades of vermillion and gilt can tinge the grey. I wished to take a holistic approach to the subject – I have tried to build a picture of this virtually unknown woman by interlocking the historical and archaeological evidence with an examination of the beliefs, influences and guiding factors she may have faced. As oral tradition survives in part in stories and legend, I have also examined the local mythology for any clues to her world.

It is hard to write a book on any aspect of Rome without thinking of the legendary Monty Python sketch. There are untold numbers of books only too happy to tell us what the Romans did for us and how they brought light to our barbarian darkness. With shades of Gordon Ramsay, after the successful application of star anise into yet another recipe, 'Civilisation – DONE!' Jones and Ereira (2006, 13) make the excellent point that we have all heard the Roman propaganda, but should not automatically accept it without question. I started this book with as few preconceived notions as possible – I come neither to praise the Romans nor to bury them. My interest lies in exploring our shared history: the merging of the old and the new worlds inherent in Cartimandua's story.

The queen of the populous Brigantes tribe ruled at a time of immense change. As the Romans invaded, tribal leaders across the country chose their path either to famous defeat or unacknowledged surrender. Cartimandua allied herself with the Empire and yet we have heard of her. Well, she is mentioned in the sources – it is strange that Cleopatra, a queen ruling Egypt in the first century BC, is a household name and yet the first documented queen to have ruled part of Britain in her own right is largely unknown by most people today. Her contemporary, Boudica, is celebrated as a 'freedom fighter' who avenged the cruel treatment of herself, her daughters and her people against a tyrannical regime. We will see that this perception of her is not entirely accurate, although it is not necessary to denigrate one queen in order to examine the life of another. Analysis of the period often mentions the two monarchs together and Cartimandua usually suffers by the comparison. She is described as a Quisling, a traitor or a collaborator, who betrayed a fellow ruler for 'brownie points' with Rome. That is one explanation of the events that occurred. Looking at the actions of another queen, Elizabeth I, we could spin a similar tale. England was not invaded at that time and yet she made alliances with stronger powers to achieve what she thought was best for her people. She could have been seen to 'betray' a fellow monarch in her beheading of Mary, Queen of Scots – an emotive interpretation which does not allow for the fact that she was safeguarding her throne. Despite the intrigue and political machinations, Elizabeth was loved by her people and is seen as one of the most successful monarchs England has ever had. It is perhaps because we have the accounts of her subjects, however, that we know of their esteem for her. There are more than two sides to every story and in the case of Cartimandua, we have only heard one. She does not appear in the sources by name until AD 51, eight years after the Roman invasion. Thus we must speculate about the early part of her life and to do that, it is necessary to examine the world in which she found herself. We will return to the Brigantian queen, but not yet.

I

Introduction

A people should know when they are conquered.

This quote from the film *Gladiator* (2000) and the scene it introduces is memorable. Many of cinema's most powerful moments embrace this idea and as an audience, we are familiar with the concept of resistance against an overwhelming force. From the slaves following Spartacus and the courage of William Wallace in *Braveheart* (1995) to Luke Skywalker and the Rebel Alliance in the hugely popular *Star Wars* saga (1977), the fight for freedom against seemingly insurmountable odds often fascinates and inspires. Whether referring to a fictitious planet or to the actual rebellions many of these stories are based upon, it is not a new notion. The people in question could be from Iraq, India, Africa, America or even Britain. In each case, the native element has had to face this prospect and each person determined his or her own response. Britain, having been invaded by an empire and in turn becoming an invading empire, has explored both sides of the debate, albeit over a considerable period of years.

The Iron Age in Britain was ended by the Roman conquest of AD 43. The Britain facing the invading force was not yet a united kingdom. There were many distinct tribal domains, with separate rulers in many cases and divergent policies. For its people to be considered 'conquered', how many of these tribes would have had to be defeated or have volunteered allegiance? From the beginning, there were elements who strongly resisted and those who welcomed the Roman presence. As always, history recorded the deeds of the stubborn and glossed over the acquiescence of the willing. The 11 tribal kings who surrendered to the Emperor Claudius (Fig. 1) are not even named in the historical sources. This date, that ended a historical period and began almost 400 years of occupation and conflict, has often been cited as the beginning of Britain's immersion into the Roman Empire. In fact, Roman troops landed on our shores some time earlier with the expeditions of Julius Caesar in 55 and 54 BC.

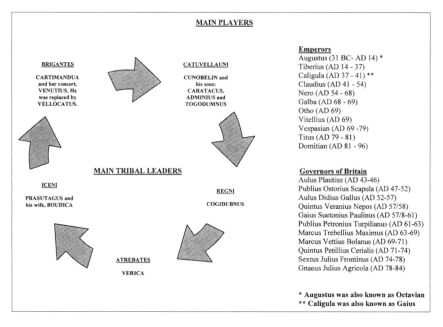

MAIN PLAYERS

BRIGANTES

CARTIMANDUA
and her consort,
VENUTIUS. He
was replaced by
VELLOCATUS.

CATUVELLAUNI

CUNOBELIN and
his sons:
CARATACUS,
ADMINIUS and
TOGODUMNUS

MAIN TRIBAL LEADERS

ICENI

PRASUTAGUS and
his wife, BOUDICA

REGNI

COGIDUBNUS

ATREBATES

VERICA

Emperors
Augustus (31 BC- AD 14) *
Tiberius (AD 14 - 37)
Caligula (AD 37 - 41) **
Claudius (AD 41 - 54)
Nero (AD 54 - 68)
Galba (AD 68 - 69)
Otho (AD 69)
Vitellius (AD 69)
Vespasian (AD 69 -79)
Titus (AD 79 - 81)
Domitian (AD 81 - 96)

Governors of Britain
Aulus Plautius (AD 43-46)
Publius Ostorius Scapula (AD 47-52)
Aulus Didius Gallus (AD 52-57)
Quintus Veranius Nepos (AD 57/58)
Gaius Suetonius Paulinus (AD 57/8-61)
Publius Petronius Turpilianus (AD 61-63)
Marcus Trebellius Maximus (AD 63-69)
Marcus Vettius Bolanus (AD 69-71)
Quintus Petillius Cerialis (AD 71-74)
Sextus Julius Frontinus (AD 74-78)
Gnaeus Julius Agricola (AD 78-84)

* Augustus was also known as Octavian
** Caligula was also known as Gaius

1 The main players

Several Roman leaders saw the merits of using the conquest of Britain to enhance their own reputation, but Julius Caesar was the first. He did not attempt either invasion unopposed, but his second campaign was met with resistance led by the tribal leader, Cassivellaunus. Native surrender resulted in the taking of hostages, the payment of tribute and the establishment of treaties. Modern thought has tended to gloss over the significance of Caesar's achievements, but it has been argued that as a result of his endeavours, the southern and eastern dynasties of Britain were established as 'friendly' or 'client' kings and although occupation was not achieved, Britain was now on the Roman radar (Creighton, 2006, 3). There is talk of British princes having 'obtained the friendship of Augustus Caesar, dedicated their offerings in the Capitol, and brought the whole island into intimate union with the Romans' (Strabo, *Geography*, 4.5.3). It is suggested that one of the ways of achieving this was the practice of educating the sons of kings in Rome – the notion of *obsides*. This has been translated as 'hostages', but the process of fostering, which was common in the ancient world, seems to be a nearer explanation. The impressionable youngsters were given an education which also encouraged the ideas and philosophies that would establish a permanent and positive link with the Empire. Classical sources support this idea as British youths were apparently noted in Rome (Strabo, *Geography*, 4.5.2) and two children in the Imperial procession on Augustus' *Ara Pacis* frieze are thought to be foreign princes.

Rome is often praised for her military skill, but it is her use of 'friendly kings' that effectively allowed her to utilise those strengths and expand her empire. She could not afford to be challenged on multiple fronts all at once and so maintained, through diplomacy, a series of buffer zones and possible intermediaries to prevent that from happening. The term 'king' or 'queen' was more likely to be used in the classical sources when Rome acknowledged a monarch. This usually meant that they were a supporter rather than an opponent; otherwise, they may have just been referred to as a chief or consort (de la Bédoyère, 2003, 76). The Roman historian, Tacitus refers to this point in describing the kings of Germany, 'in so far as Germans have any' (Tacitus, *Annals*, 13.54).

In sending their sons to Rome, the friendly kings were not anticipating just their education, but also the forming of personal connections which might strengthen their succession. Many parents today send their children away to top boarding schools in the knowledge that they will not only receive an excellent education, but that the network of contacts they will make, both within the institution and with other pupils, will stand them in good stead for life – the concept of the 'old boys' network' seems to have gone back to ancient times. Rome benefited from the friendship in terms of additional resources and manpower at their disposal, whilst reducing the threat of being attacked by enemies simultaneously. The monarchies involved gained the financial support and protection of the mighty Empire. In many cases, just being associated with Rome was enough of a deterrent against aggression and the kings avoided any interference in their kingdom as they continued to govern largely as before. In the short term, the arrangement was beneficial to both parties, but as we shall see, the friendship could often lead to annexation by the Empire. Braund (1984a, 187) argues that such friendly relationships were not deliberately created with annexation in mind, although once the kingdom was brought into the Roman universe, the possibility must have been considered by both parties. These treaties were with an individual monarch and not his kingdom, and as such, Rome had a great influence on the succession, as when the friendly king died or was overthrown, she could either annex the province if it was in her interests to do so, or threaten this course if a king she did not approve of tried to claim sovereignty (Mattingley, 2006). This may have been the reason that Augustus contemplated an expedition into Britain. However, on reaching Gaul he remained to focus on the unrest there, as 'the Britons seemed likely to make terms with him' (Dio, *Roman History*, 53.22.5).

SOURCES OF INFORMATION

The people living in Britain in the early first century AD had a largely oral tradition and there are no surviving accounts written from a native perspective from this time. Winston Churchill said that 'history is written by the victors'. In our case, the Romans were the only ones to document events for posterity, so the sources we have were written from their point of view. However, if the medieval monks had not copied the original Latin authors, nothing at all would have survived. As such, parts of the texts we have are incomplete and some contain errors – whether these were mistakes made during copying or in the original manuscripts cannot be confirmed.

Most of our information on Britain during the conquest comes from the Roman historian, Tacitus. He was thought to have been born in AD 56 or 57 and died some time after AD 115. Progressing from senatorial rank to become a provincial governor and also married to the daughter of one of the Roman governors of Britain, Tacitus forms our best literary source on the period. His *Histories* covered the years AD 69-96, but unfortunately only the years AD 68 and 69 survive. His *Annals* were written later, but detailed the earlier period from the death of Augustus in AD 14 to the death of Nero in AD 68. However, part of book V (AD 30-2) and the whole of books VII-X (AD 37-47) are missing and book XVI breaks off in AD 66, so his account of the invasion of AD 43 is lost. Writing at least 50 years after the Roman conquest, Tacitus will have relied on earlier accounts of the events and possibly even living memories as his father-in-law, Agricola, served in Britain around the time of the Boudican revolt (AD 60-1). Other Roman sources include Suetonius (born around AD 70), who must have found much of the information for his work, *The Twelve Caesars*, whilst occupying a series of posts at the Imperial Court, and the Roman senator, Cassius Dio (born in Turkey *c.*AD 150), whose *Roman History* has also not survived in full.

Ancient historians were known to place speeches in the mouths of prominent historical figures that might bear little or no resemblance to what was actually said. It was accepted practice to exaggerate the personalities of the opposing leaders, using literary devices and dramatic story-telling to emphasise the commentary on morals and character that would appeal to their intended audience and explore key issues (Salway, 1981). It is for this reason that the accuracy of these texts has been called into question. Tacitus was no exception, yet when other sources such as inscriptions have been found pertaining to a particular episode, in most cases they have supported his general narrative of events or helped us to highlight any errors (Levene's translation of the *Histories*, 1997, xi). He was not a military historian and although his work veers away from the documentary towards the literary, his opposing speeches allow us to see that his pride in the ordered rule of Rome does not blind him to her shortcomings (Wellesley, 1969, 79). Freedom and the fight for it is a common theme in Tacitus' writing and through his portrayal of the behaviour of many of the foreign rebels, he explores the virtues that he believes Rome used to have, attaching her current sins to those individuals of whom he disapproves:

> In the *Histories*, Tacitus paints the queen with a much blacker brush …
> [Cartimandua] was cruel, treacherous, scheming and immoral, all vices that
> Tacitus perceived as present in Rome and all part of the corrupting cancer of
> supreme power.
>
> Aldhouse-Green, 2006, 128

Tacitus himself says that 'so obscure are the greatest events, as some take for granted any hearsay, whatever its source, others turn truth into falsehood, and both errors find encouragement with posterity' (*Annals*, 3.19), but these very accusations are levelled at his own work. Levene (1997, xiv) points out his tendency to use rumours and innuendo and Hanson (1987, 18) cites instances where Tacitus shows individuals he dislikes in a negative light, regardless of their actions, by either 'casting aspersions as to the motivation or by the simple process of balancing any creditable behaviour with something discreditable'. He also explains that because Tacitus sees certain emperors as tyrants, he gives them all of the characteristics associated with such leaders and 'so the characterisation becomes self-fulfilling' (Hanson, 1987, 18). As he portrayed Cartimandua as a stereotypical barbarian queen, would the same apply there too? Modern leaders may baulk at the idea of being remembered thus. The American administration as portrayed by Michael Moore seems very different to official representations, but with all of the sensationalism of story-telling, it does not mean that his work is not based on fact.

The lack of any British history from this period has assisted the development of the 'painted savage' stereotype. With nothing to contradict them, classical writers were free to glorify the achievements of Roman generals and play down any possible opposition to the 'barbarian' label. Unfortunately anything put on a pedestal has a long fall to the floor. Questioning minds must have realised the dichotomy between the portrayal of Britons as naked, blue, savages who only stopped drinking mead long enough to fight each other and sleep with their sisters-in-law, and the sons of the tribal chiefs who were being sent to Rome as *obsides*. Was there a fast-track queue at the local baths to give them a de-louse, haircut and liberal spritz of 'Eau de Civilization' or did these barbarians just catch on fast? Regardless of our background though, we are all guilty of the odd xenophobic thought, especially if we support our country in international sports matches. In a situation of war and conquest, it is easy to depersonalise the people involved by making them appear vastly different, as focusing on any similarities and shared beliefs would only blur the rationale for invasion. Both nations had great strengths and obvious weaknesses – historians have chosen to focus on the former for one and the latter for the other, but recent times have shown a redressing of the balance. Iron Age and Roman historians can now play together nicely whilst discussing the superiority of Roman military strategy and the sophistication of the Coligny Calendar. The period can be explored without having to resort to extremes, especially as in reality the identities of 'Roman' and 'Briton' were probably more blurred.

RATIONALE FOR CONQUEST

> They have been invading us an inch at a time for years by invitation. There will just be more of them this time.
>
> Howarth forthcoming, *Boudica* screenplay

Events seem so much easier to understand when we can polarise the key players into good versus bad. In films, the heroes often very helpfully wear white to identify them and the villains may be ugly and awkward, but what happens when the boundaries are less well-defined and we start to challenge these labels? Maybe the Wicked Witch of the West was just misunderstood in her search for the perfect pair of shoes? Forced to wear green foundation, allergic to water and unable to have a good wash – with only the winged monkeys for company on a dull Friday night, you can see how a girl might get cranky. In history, we often simplify events by allowing a single moment to define a transition, instead of looking at a gradual chain of causality: the assassination of Archduke Franz Ferdinand is often stated as the fuse that started the First World War and the presence of Roman troops in Britain in AD 43 began the conquest. Whilst these events can be seen to be a major contributing factor and a very important part of the final outcome, there is often a build-up to such major occurrences, sometimes over many years.

Contact through trade between Rome and Britain had been long established and with the profits received from commerce, it was considered by some to be more financially advantageous not to annex the islands, rather than have to provide for the costs of occupation (Strabo, *Geography*, 4.5.3). Britain was always seen as something of an enigma, being across the mysterious Ocean, and the idea of this untapped fountain of imagined riches was ultimately too much temptation for emperors continually needing new sources of wealth. In addition, there is reason to think that they may have been given some encouragement from parties in Britain keen to manipulate the situation for their own ends.

The friendly kingdoms of the southern and eastern dynasties were largely controlled by two tribes, the Atrebates and the Catuvellauni (Fig. 2). It has been suggested that the tribes of Britain may not have adhered to the rigid groupings set out for them by the Roman writers, but we have no alternative categorisations at the present time. Based around the area that is now Hertfordshire, the Catuvellauni were a powerful tribe ruled by those who could have been the descendants of Cassivellaunus, the war leader who led the resistance to Caesar's invasion. Cunobelin was king of the eastern dynasty from the early first century AD onwards. Suetonius called him 'the British King' (Suetonius, *Caligula*, 44.2) which suggests his influence in Roman eyes, but having said that, we have already established that such a title usually reflected his approved status, rather than the scope of his domain. Even during the conquest, the Romans were far from knowledgeable about all of the powerful rulers in various quarters and just like some modern-day British southerners who ignore the existence of anything north of the Watford Gap, they presumed that any chief who had not been brought to Roman attention must not have been worth mentioning. Cunobelin, a possible *obses* in his day and whose sons may even have been educated in Rome, was king of the part that 'mattered'. His coins, a symbol of his power and status, also reflected his Roman affiliations.

The various tribal domains were prone to changing allegiances and relations between groups must have often been complicated by inter-marriages, rivalries and the expansionist policies of the ambitious. However, it was internal conflict which prompted Adminius, one of the sons of Cunobelin, to flee to the protection of Rome (Suetonius, *Caligula,* 44.2). Banished by his father, he surrendered to Caligula in Germany in AD 39 and in doing so, again reminded Rome that Britain had not yet been fully conquered. An attempt to rectify this situation was not completed and has been dismissed by the sources as a glorified seaside jaunt. Both Suetonius and Dio describe Caligula ordering his troops ashore to collect seashells as the 'spoils' of his conquest of Ocean (Dio, *Roman History* 59.25.1-3; Suetonius, *Caligula,* 46). In reality, the emperor ordered the building of a

2 Tribal map of Britain

lighthouse and began to amass troops and resources, suggesting that he had much more serious intentions. The situation was complicated by Caligula's assassination in AD 41 and the succession of his uncle Claudius to the purple. To further compound things, Cunobelin died around this period and the form of Britain's connection to the Empire was to change forever.

The Catuvellauni of the eastern dynasty were not the only ones to experience changes in their leadership. It has been suggested that free from their father's restraint and with their brother Adminius absent from any succession discussions back home, Cunobelin's other sons, Togodumnus and Caratacus began a programme of expansion that involved the southern kingdom of the Atrebates, another realm friendly to the Empire. Their king, Verica escaped to Rome, but Dio suggests that Catuvellaunian aggression was not the cause of such flight. He talks of an 'uprising' which suggests a struggle within the Atrebatian kingdom rather than an external stimulus (Dio, *Roman History*, 60.19.1). Would two potential successors to the Catuvellaunian throne have risked the displeasure of Rome by showing aggression to another neighbouring friendly kingdom or did the sons of Cunobelin not expect to have a next generation agreement with the Empire? As an emperor succeeding to an unstable regime, Claudius needed to establish his reputation and secure the loyalty of the army. A military victory would certainly begin to accomplish this goal, but was this the sole rationale behind the invasion? We are told that Claudius was 'persuaded' by Verica to send a force into Britain (Dio, *Roman History*, 60.19.1). The deposed Atrebatian king may have envisaged merely being returned to his throne in making such a request, or in gauging the feeling in Rome he could have exaggerated the 'pickings' available if annexation of the Catuvellaunian kingdom had already been decided upon. Adminius must surely have fought for his claim to Cunobelin's throne, although of the three sons mentioned in the sources, we do not know who was the eldest. His presence and that of Verica in Rome may not have been welcomed by their countrymen at this time as Suetonius describes the Britons 'threatening vengeance because the Senate refused to return certain deserters' (Suetonius, *Claudius,* 17.1). Were the British tribes likely to have baited a sleeping lion in this way or were the Roman writers attempting to justify the events of AD 43? In either case, against the background of expansionist policies and civil unrest, the decision to move troops into Britain may have been welcome in some quarters. Both the southern and eastern dynasties had benefited from their prior association with Rome, but the decision to annex British territory changed these relationships. Caratacus and Togodumnus resisted the Roman presence, but what of

Adminius and Verica? After their separate flights to Rome, both of them disappeared from the records. It is unlikely that either of them returned to the turmoil of the invasion and it has been suggested that they were either retired to an Italian city or province, or that Adminius could have been held in reserve as another possible friendly king (Creighton, 2000, 220).

THE INVASION

Of all the tribes affected by the Roman intrusion, the Catuvellauni had the most to lose. Once annexation had been decided upon, Caratacus and Togodumnus were stuck between the 'rock' of winning any skirmishes and facing the down-pouring of wrath from Rome, who could not countenance defeat, and the 'hard place' of losing to the troops occupying Britain and seeing their considerable power and status vanish overnight. Either way, their relationship with Rome was doomed, as even the humiliating thought of surrendering themselves to the mercy of the Empire had no guarantee of success. After a slow start due to mutinous troops, the Roman commander, Aulus Plautius, led his forces to victory in AD 43, although it was not with the ease he would have wished or indeed expected. After a number of encounters including a river battle (thought to have been either at the Medway or the Thames), Caratacus was forced to withdraw to the west and Togodumnus was killed. It is thought that he died at the hands of the Romans as instead of surrendering, the Britons banded together more strongly, determined to avenge his death (Dio, *Roman History*, 21.1). This has been the accepted version of events until very recently, as Hind (2007, 97) has argued that the Catuvellaunian prince did not die, but may have surrendered after being defeated. The argument hinges on the idea that the 'death' may have been of Togodumnus' resistance to Rome and that in coming to an arrangement with the enemy in defeat, his people wanted to avenge the loss of their leader to the 'other side'. So, if he did not die, what happened to him? We will answer that question shortly. However, returning to the invasion, enter Claudius and his elephants.

Opinion is divided as to why Plautius waited for his emperor's arrival before advancing to the Catuvellaunian capital of Colchester (Camulodunum). Fervent admirers of Roman military prowess have suggested that it was Claudius' desire to take credit for the victory and to be 'in at the kill' that prompted such a pause, but Dio has a different explanation. He describes Plautius as becoming frightened and deciding to practise caution as he had been instructed by Claudius to wait for reinforcements in the event of any sustained opposition (Dio, *Roman History*, 21.1-2). This could be seen to be an unfair assessment of the Roman commander's motives, but as the mutiny that delayed the advance was averted only by the intervention of Claudius sending his freedman Narcissus, it is not unthinkable that he would ask for assistance out of a tight spot again (Salway, 1981). It is understandable that individuals inclined to view the Roman war machine as nothing short of invincible would want to put a different spin on Dio's account, as hiding under the bed until 'Mother' is there to hold your hand is not really the stuff of legend. Whatever the actual reason for Plautius' decision, he did not suffer for it, as after the invasion he was governor in Britain until AD 46.

The native elite shouldered most of the burden of local administration in a province, but the main Roman concerns of maintaining order and the collection of taxes were addressed by the Imperial regime. The governor of Britain was chosen by the emperor himself, as it was considered to be one of the two most senior appointments in the occupied territories (Birley, 1981, 13). This top official had usually reached the rank of consul before being appointed to the supreme command of the legions in the province. A Roman legion had just over 5000 Roman citizen infantry soldiers, made up of cohorts of 480 men. Their numbers were bulked up by the addition of auxiliaries, who were often provincials from the lands Rome had conquered. Their unique fighting skills or horsemanship were utilised to enhance the power of the legion and after 25 years' service they were awarded Roman citizenship. The Roman writer Vegetius describes the auxiliaries as:

> ... [a] hired corps of foreigners assembled from different parts of the Empire, made up of different numbers, without knowledge of one another or any tie of affection. Each nation has its own peculiar discipline, customs and manner of fighting ... And though the legions do not place their principal dependence on them, yet they look on them as a very considerable addition to their strength.
>
> Vegetius, *The Military Institutions of the Romans*, Book II

Corruption made the levy of auxilliaries a profitable practice for some unscrupulous officials, however, as they would first choose the sons of wealthy families who could pay a bribe for their release, before taking the sons of the poor who were denied that option (Tacitus, *Histories*, 4.14). An Imperial procurator was assigned to the province to oversee taxation, but he also served as a safeguard against the governor becoming too powerful. There would have been uneasy relations between the two officers of Rome, but the potential for conflict was inherent in their differing concerns and objectives. Tacitus describes the situation from a 'British' point of view: 'we used to have one king at a time; now two are set over us – the governor to wreak his fury on our life-blood; the procurator, on our property' (Tacitus, *Agricola*, 15).

The system of friendly monarchies was expanded in Britain after the invasion, as we are told that 11 kings surrendered to Claudius at Camulodunum. Fragments of one of the arches built to commemorate his triumph state that the barbarian peoples were finally brought under Roman leadership without loss. This ignores any contribution that Caesar or even Caligula may have made, but it would not have been much of a triumph if Claudius had had to share the glory. It also suggests that some tribal leaders, having seen the results of direct resistance, decided to salvage any chance of retaining power in their own domains by ruling them on behalf of the Empire. There may have been other friendly relationships in place (apart from the southern and eastern dynasties) or being planned prior to the invasion, but as we do not know the identity of the compliant monarchs, this must remain conjecture. Such relationships would be welcomed by Rome in the immediate aftermath of the invasion, as it would allow the troops to leave domains secured by treaty and advance to conquer the areas either resistant or possibly wavering.

One of the benefits accrued by kings friendly to Rome was the grant of Roman citizenship. Some recipients did not display this badge of belonging but those that decided to did so openly. Tiberius Claudius Cogidubnus adopted the first two of his names as a tribute to his new identity. 'King' of the Regni, the sources mention that he was presented with certain other domains, as a reward for his 'unswerving loyalty' (Tacitus, *Agricola*, 14), so perhaps he was the beneficiary of the vacant Catuvellaunian and Atrebatian thrones. Here, we resume the story of the not-dead Togodumnus, as Hind (2007, 99) suggests that he and Cogidubnus could have been the same person, as 'it was Roman practice to employ defeated, but compliant, kings to rule their own states or neighbouring ones as "friendlies" '. Prasutagus of the Iceni was also confirmed as a friendly king but we do not know at what point in time. He may have had a relationship with Rome prior to the invasion or he could have been one of the 11 surrendering to Claudius. There is some thought that places his recognition later, after the Iceni rebelled in AD 47, but whether Rome acknowledged Prasutagus' status or that of his predecessor at the time of the conquest, the Iceni must have been confirmed as allies. The conquering forces moving north and west would only sensibly have done so when the tribes to their rear were either friendly or subdued by force.

Thus the events of AD 43 ended with the southern tribes facing a choice between co-operation or ruin. Rather than knowing that they were conquered, ambitious individuals could have seen this as an opportunity for advancement. Those more resistant would have to bide their time or join Caratacus away from their homes. As we have seen, there were substantially more Romans in Britain because of the invasion, but it was not some bolt from the blue; whether 'invited' by fleeing tribal princes eager to advance their own cause or merely annexing a domain whose treaty had expired with their king, Rome had been tempted with the prize of the islands beyond Ocean for too long. It was now time to fully incorporate Britain into the Empire.

WOMEN IN POWER

Rome was never ruled outright by a woman, but her empresses could wield a considerable amount of influence either through their husbands or their sons. Although the intelligence of women as a sex was never disputed, they were seen not to have the temperament or the experience to officially participate in government and public affairs (Balsdon, 1977). Dynastic marriages were a large feature of the Imperial succession and the women of the Julio-Claudian dynasty were intimately involved in the various struggles for supremacy. The sources seem to divide the empresses into two camps: those with an intense and unbecoming political interest and ambition for their sons and themselves (Livia and Agrippina) and those whose morals veered greatly away from the Roman ideal of virtue in attaining their goals (Julia, Messalina and Poppaea), but both groups were largely disapproved of by the sources. Livia was wife to one emperor and mother to another (Fig. 3). Agrippina (the Younger) was the sister of Caligula, niece and wife to Claudius and mother to Nero. Daughter of Augustus and step-daughter of Livia, Julia was married to her step-brother Tiberius. Messalina was Claudius's third wife – she was the mother of Octavia, who also married her stepbrother, Nero. After roughly 10 years of marriage, Octavia was replaced by Poppaea.

These complex relationships can be seen to be highly incestuous, both figuratively and if rumour is to be believed, occasionally literally. Slanders were reported by the sources with no suggestion of whether any truth lay behind them. However, for all of the accusations of murder and deviant behaviour, the fact remains that these women were a great influence on the politics of Imperial Rome. Livia was said to have been consulted by Augustus on many matters of state and it is suggested that on falling gravely ill in AD 37, Caligula designated his sister, Drusilla, heir to his property and,

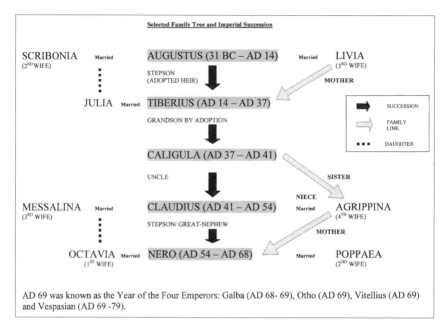

3 Imperial succession and selected family tree

more crucially, to his throne. It raised the question of whether a successor could be named by will and also the unimaginable issue of a woman being the ruler of the Empire (Bauman, 1992). Agrippina continued to push for a full partnership in power and actually achieved the unthinkable in attending a meeting of the Senate (Tacitus, *Annals*, 13.5). Informed by an astrologer when Nero was young that he would become emperor but that she would be murdered by him, the determined Agrippina is reported to have said 'Let him kill me, only let him rule' (Tacitus, *Annals*, 14.9; Dio, *Roman History*, 61.2.1-2). The main obstacles in the way of Poppaea becoming empress were Nero's mother, Agrippina, and his wife, Octavia – the former was murdered in AD 59 on the emperor's orders and the latter was divorced, watched her rival take her place on the still-warm throne and then brutally killed in exile. The beautiful red-haired and supposedly pregnant Poppaea, who excelled at manipulation and in the exploitation of her charms, added the final insult and apparently requested to see her predecessor's severed head (Tacitus, *Annals*, 14.64).

In writing about non-Roman royal women, the sources must have considered the various empresses as standards of reference. The Imperial ladies would have been at the pinnacle of possible power in their environment, but outside of Rome women ruled in various capacities and often in their own right. This would have been alien to the Roman ideal of women ruling the household and being guided by a husband or father in other more important matters. 'Barbarian' queens seemed to hold a fascination for the ancient sources, but their differences were stressed and their achievements often ignored to appeal to their largely Roman audience. Whatever their differences to the Roman women who held such great power, they are treated in a similar fashion in the records.

Those queens whose rule was largely supported by Rome are known mostly for their love lives. Cleopatra (ruling Egypt in 51 BC) is famed for her supposed relationships with both Julius Caesar and Mark Anthony. Ruling Judaea as a client queen from the mid 40s AD, Berenice of Cilicia is best known for her various failed marriages and her love affair with the future emperor, Titus. Even Cartimandua's change of consort is focused upon more than her years of faithful alliance with Rome. Those queens who opposed Rome fell into the 'unladylike' category. The Candace (Queen) of Meroe, Amanirenas, ruled modern-day Sudan in 25 BC. She led her people against the invading Roman forces and managed to negotiate a peace with Augustus. Brave, with great leadership abilities, she is described as 'a masculine woman … who had lost an eye' (Strabo, *Geography*, 17.1.54). Tacitus observed that 'Britons make no distinction of sex in their appointment of commanders' (*Agricola*, 16). In the early days of Roman conquest, Boudica was wife to Prasutagus of the Iceni, a tribe based in modern-day Norfolk. She is never referred to as 'queen' by the sources, but given that she led the rebellion against Roman rule in AD 60-1 that shook south-eastern Britain, disapproval is only to be expected. Dio calls her 'a Briton woman of the royal family' (*Roman History*, 62, 2.2), whilst Tacitus allows that she was 'a lady of royal descent' (*Agricola*, 16). It was not her origin that so offended the sources though, but the fact that she led her followers into battle. Unsurprisingly, Dio reports that 'in stature she was very tall, in appearance most terrifying, in the glance of her eye most fierce, and her voice was harsh' and just in case his audience did not grasp the point, he continues 'she now grasped a spear to aid her in terrifying all beholders' (Dio, *Roman History*, 62.2.3-4). He also describes her as a redhead, an image that has been made famous, but this could have been just another way of stressing her fiery nature. Thus, women ruling independently were either known to 'put it about a bit' or were classed as butch. But have things changed so much politically? In Britain, our one female Prime Minister was dubbed 'The Iron Lady' and jokes were made in America about President Clinton and her husband Bill, although they could actually come to fruition now.

2

The Brigantes and Conquest

(the years to AD 48)

The influence of the southern and eastern tribes in pre-conquest Britain has been well documented. However, their territory spanned relatively little of the island as a whole. In contrast, the geographer Ptolemy writing in the second century, described the lands of the northern Brigantes as 'extending to both seas' (Ptolemy, *The Geography*, 2.2). Modern definitions are slightly more precise. It is argued that Brigantia could possibly have extended as far north as Birrens in Dumfriesshire (bordering Carvetii territory) and as far south as Little Chester, near Derby (Hartley & Fitts, 1988, 5), occupying most of this area from east to west (Fig. 4). The reality is that territory was probably much more fluid than ancient sources suggest and tribal borders could have changed because of inter-marriage, treaty, trade or conflict. There is the added complication of the sources sometimes using the name 'Brigantes' as a general label for barbarians in the North. Seneca distinguishes between Britons and Brigantes (Seneca, *Apocolocyntosis*, 12) – is this another example of the North/South divide or were the Brigantes seen as separate? They could have been regarded as such, for it is assumed that the Brigantes were a federation of smaller tribal units, banded together under a single leader.

Given the geographical composition of their territory, it is understandable that smaller tribes were prevalent and that they banded together for protection. It has been suggested that the Brigantes were possibly the most powerful tribe in the region and as such gave the alliance their name. The root of the tribal name has been given several origins but whether linked to the Sanskrit 'brihati', the Gallic 'bri' or the Irish 'brig', it is generally

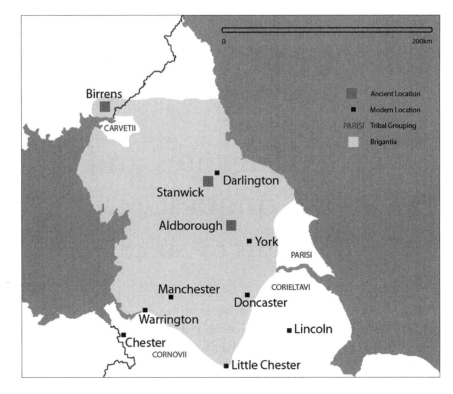

4 Map of Brigantian territory

accepted that the word means 'high' or 'exalted'. This could pertain to their geographical location in the hills and upland areas, or it may have referred to the goddess they worshipped, Brigantia. As such, Brigantia could have been a title, 'Exalted One', rather than the actual name of their goddess and so they may have been 'the people of the high one'. Hyde (1901, 53) explains that the name of the goddess 'Brigid' and the word 'goddess' were considered to be synonymous and quotes the ninth-century Irish source, *Cormac's Glossary* as evidence:

> Brigit, a goddess whom poets worshipped, for very great and very noble was her superintendence, therefore they call her goddess of poets by this name, whose sisters were Brigit, woman of healing, Brigit, woman of smith-work, i.e. goddesses, from whose names with all Irishmen Brigit was called a goddess.
>
> Cormac, king of Cashel, XXXIV

Whitley Stokes, the translator of the *Glossary*, mentions the link between the Irish Brigit and 'the Old-Celtic goddess Brigantia' (XXXIII). Brigandu, a goddess of healing, was also seen to be another counterpart, possibly worshipped by the Brigantii tribe of Gaul. In addition, there were said to be tribes with a similar name in Austria and Ireland. Did these groups all worship the same goddess, was it a title derived from similar roots of language for their own tribal protector or were the leaders of these tribes in some way related?

The goddess in a triple aspect is a common feature of pagan worship – both mother and warrior aspects protected the tribe and gave them fertility and prosperity. Altars and statues commissioned by Romans or Romanised Britons in later northern Britain show inscriptional evidence associating Brigantia with water, as at Hadrian's Wall where she is invoked as a nymph (*RIB* 2066); she is also seen as a warrior goddess linked with Victory (Castleford, West Yorkshire: *RIB* 628; Greetland, West Yorkshire: *RIB* 627) and is equated with the Roman Minerva, goddess of war, wisdom and crafts (Birrens, Dumfriesshire: *RIB* 2091). The Birrens sculpture (Fig. 5) shows

5 Stone sculpture of Brigantia from Birrens, Dumfriesshire © *National Museums Scotland. Licensor www.scran. ac.uk*

Brigantia wearing Minerva's symbol of the Gorgon's head as a pendant and a mural crown, suggesting her defence of the territory. As a warrior deity, she holds a globe of victory in her left hand, a spear in her right and has a shield behind her. It was common practice for Romans to link their gods with native deities – a process known as *interpretatio Romana* (a term derived from Tacitus, *Germania*, 43). Soldiers on campaign in a foreign land would often use a 'belt and braces' approach to religious worship – whatever their personal beliefs, they would allay any superstitions by paying some kind of homage to the powerful local gods (Ross, 1961, 85). The temple at the thermal springs of Bath was dedicated to Sulis Minerva – another pairing of local and Roman goddesses. Water was an important element in ancient native worship. Natural features such as rivers and springs were sacred and associated with fertility, the life-giving effect on crops and cattle, and the divine mother goddesses, but were also seen as an entrance to the Otherworld. Ritual deposits were offered to the gods in watery places as suggested by the number of objects found in the waters of Llyn Carrig Bach in Anglesey (Pryor, 2004, 424-7) and those found at Carlingwark Loch, Eckford and Blackburn Mill in southern Scotland (Higham, 1986).

THE HORNED GOD

The beautiful artefact pictured on the cover of the book was found at Isurium Brigantium (Aldborough) in North Yorkshire. This site was known as a *civitas*, a Romanised urban capital of a client tribe. It is thought that a fort was established there late in the first century AD, with the town beginning to emerge several years later. The piece is made from a copper alloy, possibly bronze and was enamelled originally. Unfortunately, that is the only thing that is agreed on by the archaeologists and historians. The 'horned god' is usually described as a terret, suggesting that the 'horns' are a broken part of a circular loop that would bear the reins in a chariot or wagon, guiding them from the horse's harness to the rider's hands. The terret is normally attached to a pole (yoke) and many Roman examples are 'skirted' – this would correspond to the shoulder area on our deity figure. Bishop (1996, 6) supports this assertion and dates it to the 'Celtic Renaissance' of the second century AD, rather than the pre-Roman period that the appearance of the piece may suggest. Hartley and Fitts (1988, 10-11) put forward a different explanation and include it in the pre-Roman Iron Age archaeology section of their book. They believe that the horns are actually complete and that the hole underneath could have been designed to slot the deity on top of a ritual sceptre or staff as a head-piece.

I was tremendously lucky in being able to actually handle this artefact and I have to agree with the latter authors' description of the horns as 'bovine' – in fact the whole face has that sort of look about it. Up close there is much detail that can be lost when viewing the piece in pictures or even behind the glass of the museum case. The face has a wonderful thick drooping moustache and a very strong jaw. There is a dignity about it; the suggestion that it is a depiction of an important warrior or venerated deity makes perfect sense. Various colours of enamel can still be seen and it must have been a very vibrant item in its original state. It could be a Roman piece inspired by a native deity (another example of *interpretatio Romana* perhaps), a native piece brought into a Roman military site by an auxiliary (Bishop, 1996, 3), or a pre-Roman example of a native horned god figure; it could be a sceptre head-piece or a terret. The horns are solid and terminate in smooth, nicely rounded tips – this could suggest that the horns are an original feature or, alternatively, that they could have been altered and shaped to smooth off any broken edges, if they were originally part of a ring. Whatever the explanation, this remarkable piece of the past is like much of the evidence of the tribal area from which it came and the queen who ruled there – fascinating but offering no definite answers.

The horned god, like the triple goddess, was a common representation of a local deity in pagan tribal worship for many tribes across Europe. Whether depicted with stag-antlers like the Gaulish Cernunnos (the Horned One), or with the horns of a bull or ram, as the Aldborough piece suggests, fertility and strength is implied in the attribution of these animal characteristics to the male deity (zoomorphism). This was wholly appropriate for many tribes, especially those like the Brigantes, who depended heavily on the success of the harvest and the protection of their livestock and herds for their prosperity. It is an enduring image – from the famous depiction of the stag-god on the Gundestrup cauldron found in Denmark (dated to around the first century BC) to those in the English countryside who still acknowledge Herne the Hunter. Modern-day pagans who venerate a horned god still depict him with antlers in many cases (Fig. 6). Important tribal warriors invoking the strength of this god may have shown their loyalty in fashioning horns on their headdresses as a tribute (Ross, 1961, 73) – such a 'helmet' (dating back to the Iron Age) was found in the River Thames at Waterloo Bridge. The head was said to be very important in pagan antiquity and it has been suggested that there was a belief that the

6 Twentieth-century depiction of Cernunnos, the Horned God. © *P. Borda 1997*

soul was to be found there (Berresford Ellis, 1990). Thus, the representation of the horned god as a head could indicate the significance of the piece. Some ancient tribes were said to have decapitated their enemies and kept the skulls as trophies – a custom which Romans found distasteful and so were obviously keen to write about. None of the classical sources refer to such a practice in Britain, but some archaeological evidence may support this idea. In excavating Stanwick, a late Iron Age complex in North Yorkshire, in the early 1950s, Sir Mortimer Wheeler found a sword still in its scabbard near to a decapitated head, outside the site defences. It was suggested that both finds could have been part of a trophy, with the head having been attached to the gate-structure itself or placed on a pole by the entrance (Wheeler, 1954, 53).

CARTIMANDUA'S CAPITAL?

The fortified site at Stanwick, near Darlington, North Yorkshire, seems well-placed as a focus for tribal communication as it stands between the Rivers Tees and Swale, close to the intersection of two major Roman roads. Both were said to have been built on pre-existing routes: the north–south Dere Street (now the A1) and the north-western cross-Pennine route which is now the A66 (Fig. 7). The Stainmore Gap provided an approach to the Eden Valley and Cumbria and as such, Stanwick was ideally located to control the northern Brigantes (Ramm, 1980, 28). The complex itself occupies an area of almost 3 sq km (290ha) inside the earthworks, which themselves stand to a height of more than 16ft (5m) in places. Dimensions aside, this highly impressive structure has been the source of much debate regarding its exact Brigantian heritage and the dating of the site.

It is necessary to pre-empt our story somewhat and briefly outline the turbulent events in Brigantian history which could have been linked in some way to this location. Relying solely on Tacitus for this chronology, we are concerned with a documented period AD 47-74. The Roman author describes a brief uprising in AD 47-8 and then concentrates on two more important rebellions in Brigantia in this time frame. It has been suggested that the two separate narratives (one in the *Annals* and one in the *Histories*) could relate to the same rebellion, a theory that will be examined in detail later, but for now we will treat the two episodes as independent. The first was said to have occurred some time between AD 51 and AD 57, and the second in AD 69. The initial revolt followed the divorce of the royal couple, Cartimandua and Venutius, an event which led to the tribal consort abandoning his previously pro-Roman stance and invading the kingdom, only to be defeated by Roman troops coming to the aid of the queen. The ensuing rift between them lasted for more than a decade and culminated in Cartimandua being rescued by Roman forces for a second time and Venutius assuming control of the throne. This victory was short-lived, however, as his subsequent fight against the advancing Roman Army was futile and the Brigantian rebels were defeated by the forces of the governor Petillius Cerealis in AD 71-4.

Returning to Stanwick, archaeologists have begun to appreciate that the finds recovered and the defences uncovered there have posed as many questions as they answered about the history of the complex. Wheeler excavated the site in three main phases in his work there in 1951-2. Phase I began with the nucleus of the complex, The Tofts 'hillfort', which he dated as occupied by the native population by the mid first century AD.

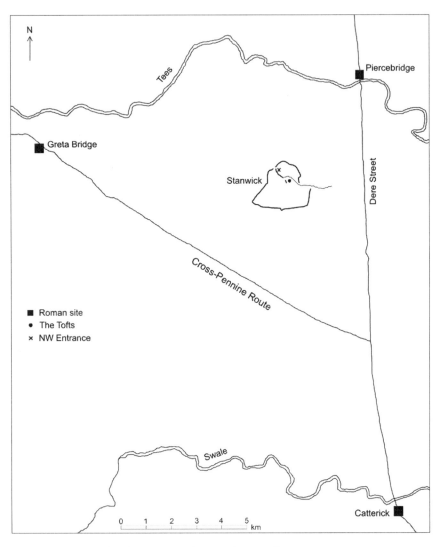

7 Map of Stanwick fortifications. *Based on Haselgrove et al, 1990*

Phases II and III extended the enclosure considerably in his view and he dated them as *c.*AD 50-60 and post AD 69 respectively (Wheeler, 1954, iii; 18-21). As Wheeler believed Stanwick to have been Venutius' stronghold, it was suggested that Phase II of the extension of the earthworks was in response to the continuing hostilities after the first rebellion. Phase III was then related to the events after the overthrow of Cartimandua in AD 69 and Venutius' subsequent stand against the Romans in AD 71-4.

Further excavations of Stanwick were undertaken in 1981-9 by Colin Haselgrove and his colleagues, and their findings supported prior challenges to Wheeler's timeline of events. Evidence including high-status Roman imported 'finewares' suggested an important late Iron Age settlement at Stanwick pre-dating Wheeler's 'Phase I occupation'. As only a small area of the entire site has been examined in detail, and given the multi-period nature of the evidence, it is difficult to be certain of the precise chronology, but Haselgrove *et al* (1990, 86-7) propose that the earlier settlement was comfortably organised and enjoying luxury items from the south by the mid first century AD, when the monumental earthworks were built in a reasonably short period of time and many buildings in the interior re-constructed. As part of this research, the famous 'Stanwick' hoard was re-examined and new information obtained. Discovered in 1843, the collection was assumed to have been found within the Stanwick earthworks, but the find spot was actually a kilometre away on a farm in Melsonby. The well-known horse's head mask (which can be seen along with other parts of the hoard in the British Museum) may have formed part of the decoration on a large iron-bound wooden tub or bucket, possibly stripped before deposition in the ground. The Melsonby site was linked to Stanwick through their shared exceptional status and their history, as both were connected to the period of Brigantian friendship with Rome in the first century AD. The burn marks on some of the items suggested that the hoard may have come from a large funerary chamber and had passed through the flames of the pyre, and the dismantling of the bucket before being put in the ground could suggest a ritual deposition, but it is equally possible that the weaponry, horse harness, chariot fittings and other metalwork could have come from a workshop (Fitts *et al*, 1999, 48).

Stanwick was at the height of its prosperity at a time when Brigantia was a kingdom friendly to Rome and as such it is possible that Cartimandua and not her troublesome ex could have been based there. The large and imposing north-western entrance seems designed as much to impress as to protect and the high-status imports would have added to the prestige of such a palatial dwelling. Haselgrove (1989, 385) describes many of the imported finds as 'extremely unusual: rare Samian forms, uncommon amphora varieties, and volcanic glass hardly known outside Italy; they have the look more of diplomatic gifts than normal trade goods'. To be able to erect such a vast construction relatively quickly suggests that the ruling power had command of enough manpower and resources to organise such a task. These *oppida* (fortified settlements) were often centres of trade, communication and expressions of political power and wealth:

> if Stanwick was the seat of power of someone who achieved exceptional status
> … people would have been drawn there in large numbers: other members of
> the Brigantian elite and their entourages, craft workers dependant on wealthy
> patronage who fashioned prestige metalwork like that in the Stanwick hoard;
> ambassadors and traders, or those who owed services and tribute.
>
> Haselgrove, 1989, 385

The defences were so vast as to be hard to protect from a sustained attack, but co-operation with Rome would have rendered such considerations less important. This could be why Cartimandua had to be rescued after the events of AD 69, as her capital may not have been able to be defended efficiently from a prolonged invasion. Wheeler suggested that Stanwick had been overrun by Roman forces in defeating Venutius, but evidence of such strife is not visible from the evidence uncovered so far. Instead it is postulated that the immense structure was allowed to fall into disrepair rather than being deliberately destroyed in warfare.

BRIGANTIAN ECONOMY

Romanisation is often seen as the gradual process of cultural transplant, with the ruling elite passing changes down to the native population. As Britain was not a united kingdom but made up of different tribal groupings, each with their own traditions, commerce and settlements, there will have been no general response to an invading force. Each area will have had a tribal aristocracy with different aims and ambitions. Areas in the north will have reacted differently than their southern neighbours and rural highland areas will not have had the same experience as an urban population. Via contact with Rome through trade and the early establishment of friendly kingdoms, Britain will have seen a gradual blending of the old and the new. The consumption of imported luxury items such as pottery, glass and wine has often been linked to the adoption of Roman values and practices.

Rather than the trappings of adopting a new way of life, it could be that these items were prized not for their difference to native items, but because they were similar to goods already considered to be desirable. Romans were renowned for taking a good idea and improving on it, so whether they were walking on straighter roads, eating out of ceramic bowls instead of wooden ones or drinking wine instead of ale, the Britons could appreciate such improvements without the wholesale adoption of a different culture:

> It looks as though the cognitive and social significance of imported wine and associated objects in Iron Age Europe has been rather overdone because of a failure to conceptualise the people involved on the other, non-Roman, side of the relationship as possessing coherent, resilient, but changing cognitive worlds able to assimilate and reinterpret imports on their own terms.
>
> Williams, 2005

The Brigantian elite had the high-status complex at Stanwick, but many of the major changes in architecture, town planning and urbanisation occurred once the territory was annexed by Rome after Cartimandua's overthrow and Venutius' defeat. The presence of the army would have stimulated local trade, both increasing and generating demand for goods and services. Brigantia would have had a mainly pastoral economy, with the lowlands more able to rely on agriculture. As a society basing its wealth on the ownership of fertile land, its main exports are likely to have been hides and wool. Mining for lead and exploiting the local stone and clay will have also proved profitable.

COINS

The Romans did not institute coinage in Britain as is sometimes believed. Native coins were being minted in Kent as early as 100 BC (Pryor, 2004, 421) and foreign coins appeared in Britain quite some time before that. Their uses in ancient society extended way beyond payment for goods and services and storing wealth. Gold coins in particular were used to indicate power and status – these prestige items were used as gifts among the elite, for special purposes such as dowry payments and tributes, and for ritual deposition to propitiate the gods (Creighton, 2000, 14, 30, 226). Coins could tell the people of a shift in leadership, with the changes in symbolic imagery in some cases underlining the very nature of kingship itself. Dynastic marriage and interaction with Rome and other friendly kings was also reflected in the visual representations on coins. There is extensive evidence of the southern and eastern dynasties' coinage but what of the northern kingdom of the Brigantes?

Gold and silver staters, bearing the name VOLISIOS on the obverse and the partial CARTI–VE… on the reverse, were found in West Yorkshire in the nineteenth century. Having been uncovered in her territory, and bearing the partial element (CARTI) of her name, they were originally attributed to Cartimandua. It is suggested that the coins date to the early part of the first century AD as Richmond (1954, 47) believed the issues to have been minted before Cartimandua began her friendly relationship with Rome. Volisios was thought to have been an early Brigantian leader, who was eventually succeeded by the tribal queen. The second element –VE was believed to have referred to Venutius. A gold stater bearing the same inscriptions was found more recently in 1999 (CCI no. 99.0827; Fig. 8). The evidence has now been reinterpreted and in studies of the distribution pattern, the coins were shown not to be Brigantian but probably belonging to the Corieltavi tribe (Allen, 1963, cited in Hanson & Campbell, 1986, 74). CARTIVE was thought to relate to Cartivellaunos, a Corieltavian leader possibly sharing power with Volisios.

In the light of this reattribution, it would appear that there were no Brigantian coins. It could be that none have yet been found and recognised as such. As happened with the Corieltavian coins, modern study is constantly reinterpreting past conclusions. If Cartimandua did mint coins, they could have been melted down and used for other purposes in the uprisings that tore Brigantia apart. The kingdom obviously had access to coinage, as a few were found in the 1980s excavation of Stanwick, and as an ally of Rome, coins may have been one of the gifts often lavished on co-operative monarchs. There are numerous possibilities, but on current evidence it would appear that none were minted in the region. Friendly monarchs were perfectly able to produce coins during Roman rule, but whether or not she had the privilege, Cartimandua may not have had the desire to do so.

The Brigantes may have had their own system of exchange to which coinage had no relevance. Everything from sword blades in ancient Britain to whales' teeth in Fiji has been used as a means of payment and barter. Like that of the Kikuyu tribe in Africa, and those of some parts of Wales and Ireland, the pastoral communities in Brigantia may have used cattle as a form of currency. Hides and wool or even the animals themselves could have been exchanged for luxury items without the need for actual coins. Higham (1993) suggests that local farmers could have sold their produce

8 Volisios Cartivellaunos gold stater – CCI 99.0827 © *Institute of Archaeology, University of Oxford*

in the towns for cash to pay any necessary taxes and then exchanged any remaining coins for goods before returning home – this would explain the finding of bangles and pottery on some farm sites. It is possible that there were not enough readily available metals to mint coinage and as a friendly monarch, Cartimandua may even have been provided with Roman coins to distribute. Chariots and a team of trained horses may have been part of the system of exchange among the elite (Creighton, 2005), for, as shown by their numerous representations on British coins, these noble animals were evidently important in symbolising tribal power and wealth.

BRIGANTIAN ROYALTY

Cartimandua was a hereditary ruler – she did not marry into the royal family, but was a 'princess of high birth' (Tacitus, *Histories*, 3.45.1). It has been suggested that her predecessor could have unified the diverse tribes of Brigantia, which would explain why her lineage was considered to have been so powerful (Hartley & Fitts, 1988, 2). Another possibility is that a dynastic marriage cemented an alliance between tribal units. Cartimandua's consort, Venutius, was a Brigantian – in describing the events of the AD 50s, Tacitus refers to an earlier mention of this fact, which unfortunately has not survived. As part of the missing books of the *Annals*, this allusion could have been in the periods AD 30-2 or AD 37-47. It is not known which original tribal group Venutius came from, but it has been suggested that he could have been one of the people later known as the Carvetii. In describing the Brigantian resistance to Rome, Wheeler spoke of the 'tribes rallying from the north and north-west – from those borderlands whence most of the auxiliary tribesmen of Venutius must have come' (1954, 25). Birley (1973, 188), having cited the references to the separate *civitas* of the Carvetii (*RIB* 933; Wilson & Wright, 1965, 224), also refers to this tribe as being part of 'Venutius's forces'. Whether originating from this tribal area or merely forming an alliance with them in his resistance against Rome, Venutius' claim to sovereignty was subordinate to that of his wife. As Cartimandua was the queen and not a consort, it suggests that she came from the more powerful of the two groups or that she succeeded an existing ruler.

In placing the earlier reference to Venutius, a certain amount of supposition is necessary. Romans considered girls to be ready for marriage at the age of 12 and boys at the age of 14. However, it is thought that girls in the provinces did not approach matrimony at such a young age. Caesar comments that intercourse with a girl under 20 was considered to be shocking (*De Bello Gallico*, 6.21), supported by Tacitus who noted that girls in Germany were 'not hurried into marriage' (*Germania*, 20). Tombstone evidence from Britain also suggests that many girls postponed marriage until at least their early 20s (Allason-Jones, 2005, 22), but political marriages may have defied such traditions. Tacitus' narrative of the years AD 37-47 in the *Annals* did not survive and as he never mentions the Brigantian alliance thereafter, it is plausible to believe that Cartimandua was married at some point in this missing period. Supposing that she was 20 in AD 43, she could have been married to Venutius for anything up to eight years if her family had observed the Roman age of consent. This would fit in with the missing years in Tacitus' work and give a possible timeline to work with. The Roman conquest could have acted as a stimulus for such a tribal amalgamation (Turnbull & Fitts, 1988, 382), but it cannot be known why Venutius is mentioned in the earlier Tacitean source. He cannot have been one of the 11 kings surrendering to Claudius, even if he had been king of his own tribe prior to marrying Cartimandua. Although Venutius is later said to have had long-standing loyalty to Rome, it is linked to his marriage to the tribal queen (Tacitus, *Annals*, 12.40) and it would have been Cartimandua and not her consort who made any treaties with Rome. Wheeler suggests that the initial mention of Venutius could have been in describing the Brigantian uprising in AD 47-8 (1954, 20), but as Tacitus already mentions this unrest in the *Annals* with no naming of any key individuals, it would suggest that the missing reference concerns an earlier period.

TRIBAL UPRISING

Richmond (1954, 47) suggests that Cartimandua was queen of the Brigantes before the invasion of AD 43 and that in acknowledging her sovereignty, the emperor was showing recognition of an existing status. Tacitus supports the view of Cartimandua having been an established monarch by the time of the conquest. As previously mentioned, he describes her husband's extended loyalty to Rome prior to their divorce in the 50s AD, and before describing the capture of Caratacus in AD 51, he explains that Cartimandua had ruled the Brigantes for some time (Tacitus, *Histories*, 3.45). It is uncertain whether the queen actually had a client relationship with Rome (Turnbull & Fitts, 1988, 383), but there was certainly some sort of treaty in place benefiting both parties. Frere (1987) believes the relationship to have been unique: 'Cartimandua was in a class by herself, for her Brigantian kingdom lay beyond the frontiers of the province and was not really under Roman control save at the cost of special military effort'. The queen had the strength of Roman arms to support her throne, which was to prove very useful on several occasions and the Romans had the co-operation of the vast Brigantian kingdom, which allowed them to focus on their campaign in the south-west unhindered. This arrangement prevented sympathetic northern tribes sending reinforcements or providing areas of possible retreat and thus avoided conflict on multiple fronts for the Romans.

Having seen all possible south-eastern allies crushed by the invasion or volunteering to pay homage to Rome, Caratacus retreated to Wales. There is no evidence of any treaty or kinship between the Welsh tribes and his own people, yet the Catuvellaunian rebel prince was able to win the support of the Silures in his hostility to Rome. It is unlikely that he would have brought enough followers with him to coerce such an outcome. The mountain tribes must have had their own leaders and objectives, and yet Caratacus was able to gain passage through their lands and bring these people to his side. They may already have been resistant to the idea of Roman advance and Caratacus could have been a very persuasive and charismatic figure, but it is possible that the Druids helped to establish him as a leader so quickly. These powerful religious figures, forced to leave their sanctuaries by the invasion, could have used their political influence amongst the tribes to unite them under one war-leader (Webster, 1993b, 57).

Facing Caratacus' hostile tribes in AD 47, as they had decided to take advantage of the newly appointed governor and the prospect of winter coming to attack the outskirts of the province, Ostorius Scapula put down all initial resistance and then decided to disarm all 'suspect' tribes on the

Roman side of the Severn-Trent border (Tacitus, *Annals,* 12.31). Claudius had removed weapons from all conquered territory after the invasion and the allied tribes were bound by treaty, but at this unsettled time, the removal of arms was extended past those hostile to Rome or possibly undecided on their course, to even the friendly tribes. Thus having volunteered their co-operation to the Roman forces, these allied tribes were subjected to rigorous searches and the degradation of having their weapons confiscated – a move engendering anti-Roman feeling in all. Webster (1993a, 21-22) suggests that this could have been a deliberate move by Ostorius Scapula to identify any trouble zones, as those in open defiance of this decree could be targeted and immediately dealt with. The first to react were the Iceni, who had been previously been content to ally themselves with Rome – they were joined by neighbouring tribes which are not named by Tacitus, but it has been suggested that it could have been the Corieltavi and the Catuvellauni (Webster, 1993b, 59). The revolt was quickly crushed, with the client kingdom remaining intact. Prasutagus was king of the Iceni in AD 60, which suggests that either he succeeded to the throne after the events of AD 47 or that he was king before the revolt, but clearly had no part in the resistance against Rome.

In AD 48, disturbances among the Brigantes tested the understanding with Rome and brought the new governor, Ostorius Scapula back from his campaign against the Deceangli in Wales. It is likely that there were several contributing factors to the cause of this unrest. Higham suggests that the death of a king, acknowledged as ruler of the Brigantes between AD 43 and AD 47 and leaving no male heirs, caused the tribal tensions that beckoned the governor back from the west. He argues that questions about the future of the kingdom were answered, as the queen had the backing of her loyal and militarily astute husband and this would have given Ostorius Scapula 'sufficient confidence in Cartimandua both to allow and to recognise her succession' (Higham, 1987, 11). How fortunate that Venutius was around, for as Boudica showed when she mobilised a couple of people against the Romans, British women were helpless without their men-folk! Another view suggests that it was Aulus Plautius and not his successor who was to 'place Queen Cartimandua on the throne of Brigantia' (Webster, 1993a, 13). These are both interesting theories, but there is no evidence to support either one of them. A Roman governor would certainly not have had the authority to settle a matter of tribal succession – the emperor would have decided whether to recognise a monarch (Braund, 1984a, 26). Cartimandua may well have succeeded a ruler with no male heirs, but this would have had no bearing on her claim to the throne. As we have already heard from

Tacitus, the British had no problem with female command and Venutius actually gained his status by being married to Cartimandua and not the other way around.

There is no suggestion that the rising was against Roman rule or that they had been threatened with disarmament, but the tension within the tribal alliance could have followed Cartimandua's co-operation with the Empire. The size of the Brigantian territory and the number of prominent nobles would have meant that rival factions, each with their own aims and agendas, would have been inherent in such a vast kingdom. As leader of the individual sub-tribes, Cartimandua must have struggled to enforce any common policy, especially one with such far-reaching consequences for all involved. Her decision to commit her kingdom to such a course of action may have been unpopular with certain factions whose sympathies lay with the uprising of the Iceni and especially with the resistance of certain Welsh tribes in AD 47. Frere (1987) suggests that some of the south-western branches of the Brigantes had close ties with the border regions of the Welsh Marches. They reacted strongly once Ostorius Scapula began his conquest of the Deceangli and Cartimandua's control of this area of her lands could have been compromised by the distance from her main seat of power (Turnbull & Fitts, 1988, 378).

Certain factions may wish to have given their support to Caratacus in his continued fight against the Empire. It is also proposed that in using tribal labour to build the vast fortifications at Stanwick, any anti-Roman sentiment would have been intensified; resentment could have been caused as workers and resources were redeployed to construct this symbol of prestige and alliance with Rome (Higham, 1987, 17). Whatever the cause of the tribal grievances, Ostorius Scapula had no obligation to get involved in this matter unless a treaty was already in existence. According to Tacitus, the Roman commander did not wish to undertake new endeavours before concluding his previous business (Tacitus, *Annals*, 12.32). The fact that he left Deceanglian territory whilst in sight of reaching of his goal there shows how crucial Brigantian security was to Rome. In honouring the terms of an agreement designed to protect Cartimandua's throne, he would also stamp out any threats to his flank whilst campaigning in Wales. Rome would no doubt have considered any challenge to their allies as resistance against the Empire and would have intervened accordingly. In this case, the death of the ringleaders and the pardon of the rest allowed the matter to be settled quickly. Like Prasutagus, Cartimandua survived the minor uprising of her people with no change to her relationship with Rome. The royal household is not mentioned in conjunction with the incident, reinforcing the idea that they played no part in the events that occurred. It has also been proposed that as Cartimandua was not included in Tacitus' account of the trouble, it 'suggests not that she became queen thereafter, but that she was already queen, for her accession is not mentioned in the extant books of Tacitus' (Braund, 1996, 197, n.14), supporting the theory that her sovereignty predated the invasion.

3

Caratacus, Venutius and the Boudican Rebellion

(AD 51-60)

The intervention of Rome in the Brigantian unrest of AD 48 would have changed Cartimandua's position in her kingdom. If the queen had made an early treaty with the Empire, her people did not show any displeasure for some time. The resistance shown by the Iceni and their neighbours, and the Welsh tribes who rallied around Caratacus, may have acted as a catalyst for any anti-Roman feeling among the Brigantes to explode into action, but it was immediately apparent that such behaviour would not be tolerated. The perception of the queen's power and influence would have changed drastically now that Rome had entered the territory in a military capacity. Groups who had not initially objected to a treaty with the Empire may have come to realise that the queen had powerful reinforcements at her disposal.

There is no evidence that Cartimandua asked for aid in restoring the peace. Ostorius Scapula's decision to intervene in the matter could have been a signal to any neighbouring tribes wavering between resistance and compliance, to the anti-Roman factions in Brigantia, but also to the queen herself. She would have realised in no uncertain terms that Rome expected total loyalty. If Ostorius Scapula returned from Wales on his own initiative, Cartimandua must have known that any suggestion of a threat to the Roman flank would be dealt with immediately. If she was to retain control in her realm and not give the Empire any excuse to consider her lands part of the province, she would have to ensure that her people did not challenge her political allegiances. The ringleaders of the uprising were killed, although the rest were shown lenient treatment – maybe Cartimandua actually dealt with these rebellious subjects herself to reinforce the idea that her authority

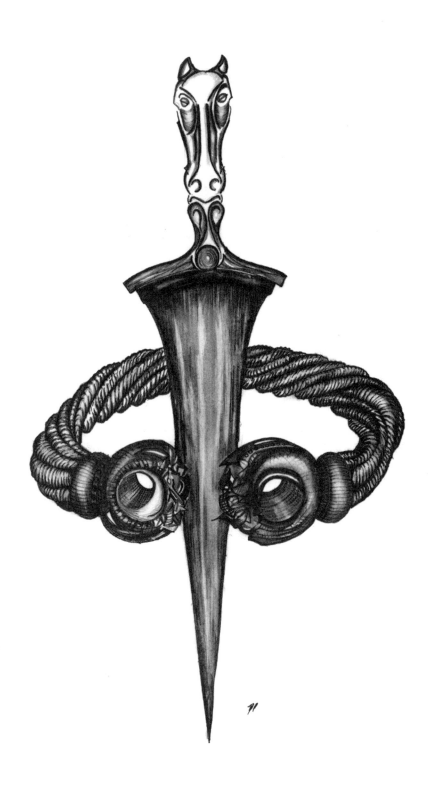

was not to be questioned. Ostorius Scapula would surely not have risked a campaign into Wales without the guarantee of security at his back.

The queen was useful to Rome in providing this stable frontier to safeguard Roman conquest elsewhere – warring elements in her kingdom may change such a perception. In the aftermath of the trouble, Cartimandua would surely have stressed to her tribal leaders that alliance with Rome was no guarantee of special treatment. Brigantia had not been disarmed before the uprising and there is no suggestion that such steps were taken afterwards, but the client kingdom of the Iceni, who had volunteered their alliance to Rome without the need for conquest, had been included in the 'suspect tribes' and had their weapons removed. Such a move by Ostorius Scapula would seem politically rash – after all, the Iceni only rebelled in response to such treatment – but allies or not, the governor could have had his suspicions about the loyalty of certain tribal factions. After the revolt, the Iceni continued their friendly agreement with Rome for some years under the leadership of Prasutagus.

The disarming of the tribes would have had far-reaching consequences for the social structure of the community. It is likely that many ancestral blades and shields, passed down from father to son, were hidden from the Imperial searches, but the right to carry a weapon would have formed part of the tribal mentality. Warriors in the tribe who may have offered their services to the chief as a form of tribute not only lost the tools of their trade, but were replaced in their military role by full-time professional soldiers. This reduction of status to the class of civilian, peasant or farmer (if they had other, less military-orientated skills) must have been devastating. For those unable to change their calling, service in foreign lands must have beckoned and those without families or strong affinities to their home may have even enlisted in the Roman Army as auxiliaries and been sent overseas. Higham (1993) makes the excellent point that the disarming of the tribes would have meant that they were 'shorn of the warrior characteristics that were arguably a crucial component of pre-Roman British religion'. How would those who worshipped a warrior deity be able to rationalise such a change in their self-perception and the way others may have perceived them? Rebellion may have been the only avenue open to those who did not want to believe that their gods had forsaken them.

Caratacus had chosen well in rousing the Welsh Silures to revolt. They proved to be Rome's toughest and most successful opponents in Britain, using the nature of the terrain and knowledge of their territory to their best advantage (Frere, 1987). Tacitus describes how their fierceness was strengthened by the belief in their leader's abilities – his many military successes allowing him to rise to prominence (Tacitus, *Annals*, 12.33). Anticipating the Roman penetration of Silurian lands, Caratacus moved the focus of resistance north to the Ordovician region to avoid being surrounded. In AD 51, he took a defensive position in the steep hills of Snowdonia behind a river with no easy crossings, where smoother slopes were blocked by piled stones. Roman cavalry could not operate freely in the densely wooded terrain, but after a struggle the infantry broke through and won a pitched battle. Caratacus' wife and daughter were captured and his brother surrendered (Tacitus, *Annals*, 12.35). A great war-leader he may have been, but Caratacus would not win the 'Husband of the Year' award. Undaunted by the seizure of his family, he made for Brigantia, retreating through the gap that Ostorius Scapula had hoped to cut off in his unfinished campaign in North Wales. The battle had been lost, but the Silures continued to fight the war, apparently enraged by rumours of the governor's oath to exterminate the entire tribe (Tacitus, *Annals*, 12.39).

There are many explanations for the rebel leader's flight into pro-Roman territory. Caratacus may have had some dealings with the Brigantian queen if only in a trading capacity. Salway (1981) describes how prior to the invasion, the Catuvellauni may have been able to supply or withhold high-status goods and luxury items desired by the leaders of other British tribes pretty much at will. Welsh legend tells that Cartimandua (named as Aregwedd Foeddawg in the Triads) and Caratacus were second cousins, whereas the Scots (in *The Buik of the Croniclis of Scotland*, Turnbull, 1858) believed Cartimandua to have been the rebel leader's stepmother (Casson, 1945, 71 and 76). There could have been some familial links though inter-marriage between the Brigantian and Catuvellaunian dynasties, but there is no evidence to prove it. As Cartimandua captured Caratacus and handed him over to the Romans, imagining a relationship between them only extends the drama and attempts to paint the queen in a blacker light, but it is equally possible that the two royals had nothing at all to do with each other. If there had been some connection between them, in a desperate situation, the warlord may have believed that he would have been given sanctuary, but it is unlikely. Brigantia was known as a pro-Roman territory, especially after the events of the uprising only a few years before. It is more probable that he wished to raise support amongst the anti-Roman factions and continue his fight from there.

Cartimandua has been called many names for her treatment of Caratacus – Quisling, traitor, collaborator and betrayer of a fellow ruler. These are emotive labels that do not take account of the queen's situation. Vidkun Quisling was a Norwegian politician who helped the Nazis to conquer his own country in World War II. His name is used as a synonym for traitor or collaborator. In law, treason is the crime of disloyalty to, or betrayal of, one's nation. The Brigantian queen did not belong to a nation – Britain was made up of a number of independent tribes – so can Cartimandua technically be guilty of treason? Far from trying to help a foreign party conquer her people, she was attempting to stop them from being immersed in the Empire. Her actions may have benefited her personally and meant that she retained her throne, but she also managed to keep her lands as an independent kingdom. We do not know of any objections to Cartimandua's rule before her alliance with Rome – the nature of freedom will be discussed later on, but it is quite possible that the Brigantian people benefited from their queen's political manoeuvring.

Collaboration may be defined as co-operation with enemy forces occupying one's own country – Cartimandua certainly assisted the Romans in their expansion elsewhere in Britain, but there is no evidence that they ever occupied her kingdom whilst she ruled and although other tribes undoubtedly suffered by her liaison with Rome, her own people remained largely unmolested. McNeill (1998) defines Hoffman's idea (1968) of the *collaboration d'état* or 'State collaboration' of France during the Second World War as 'a pragmatic political and economic co-operation with Nazi Germany with the immediate aim of safeguarding French interests and the longer-term aim of securing a better position for France in a post-war Europe dominated by Germany'. He differentiates this from the type of collaboration shown by letters of denunciation, in which the local people were encouraged to identify members of the Resistance, sympathisers and Jews to the authorities and were often used as a way of settling personal scores. This kind of behaviour may have occurred in occupied Britain, but Cartimandua could hardly be accused of practising it. She did not seek out Caratacus, but handed him over to the Romans once he threatened the stability and security of her kingdom – she did not want her people to suffer the reprisals he faced for his actions in fighting the governor's troops. The Brigantes were not going to be another tribe he left to face the consequences of defeat whilst he went off to find other means of support.

Cardinal Richelieu once said that 'to mislead a rival, deception is permissible; one may use all means against his enemies'. In order for her to 'betray' Caratacus, Cartimandua would have had to practise some sort of deception in cultivating a relationship for an ulterior purpose before the inevitable violation of trust (Jackson, 2000, 85). Given Cartimandua's pro-Roman tendencies, it is much more likely that any possible connection with Caratacus would be ignored in the light of his persistent rebellion against the Empire, rather than encouraging an association in the hope that it would prove beneficial. There may have been some blood tie between them, but there is no suggestion of any sustained interaction between the two leaders. Justified or not, there is nothing to hint at the fact that Caratacus was tricked into capture either – a man famed for his cunning and tactical skill would surely not have fallen for a ruse from a monarch known for her support of Rome.

It is equally possible that there was no bond between them at all and that Caratacus fled to the kingdom in the hope of gaining reinforcements to continue his fight against the governor. He would have been aware of the recent uprising and probably relied on persuading any discontented elements to join with him in rebellion against the Empire, against the express wishes of the queen, and in doing so seriously endangering her position with Rome. In such a scenario, when her throne, her position and the success of her treaty with Rome was at stake, it is not surprising that Cartimandua removed this threat and assured her allies of her loyalty. The move is not likely to have been popular amongst her subjects, but many monarchs have had to sacrifice being liked because they wished to be feared and respected. Elizabeth I took the difficult decision to execute Mary, Queen of Scots, as she knew that her cousin had been plotting to remove her from the throne with the help of Catholics in and beyond her realm. Caratacus could have threatened more than has been initially proposed – he had gained control of the Welsh Silures and Ordovices and been appointed their leader. With certain elements in the tribal alliance disillusioned enough to take up arms, perhaps Caratacus believed that he could lead the Brigantes, regaining some of his former power and status as head of such a vast kingdom. He had no problem with leaving his family to be captured by the advancing Roman Army, so taking over the throne of someone who may have been a distant relation would have been no great sacrifice, as he was determined to succeed at all costs. His actions in retreating to Brigantia could have been the last resort of a desperate man, but there must have been far more sympathetic and certainly much nearer boltholes to flee to. Tacitus observed that 'the defeated have no refuge' (Tacitus, *Annals*, 12.36) – had Caratacus been successful in Wales, it is unlikely that he would have approached Cartimandua for support as her position would have been seriously compromised and even if he had, she would still undoubtedly have refused to help. If Ostorius Scapula had been beaten, the Empire could not have allowed a defeat to go unpunished and the might of Rome would have descended on Britain as an example to any other would-be rebels.

The capture of Caratacus was regarded as a great victory in Rome. He was a respected adversary with a far-reaching reputation after many years of defying Roman authority and his presence in the capital as part of Claudius' triumphal parade drew great crowds. Tacitus, of course, gives Caratacus a stirring speech – it had to be good as the emperor is supposed to have reacted to it by pardoning the rebel and his family (Tacitus, *Annals*, 12.37). Released from their bonds, the grateful Britons, examples of Imperial mercy, showed the same gratitude and homage to both Claudius and his wife, Agrippina. Much is made of this episode by the Roman authors. They are critical of the forward behaviour of the empress in being seated separately before the Roman standards and flaunting herself as a partner in the Empire. However, it also serves to further emphasise the attitude of the British nobility to a woman in power: 'not only could a woman be a leader in her own right but the female consort of a ruler was of equal importance and entitled to respect' (Allason-Jones, 2005, 7).

As shown by the impressive display at Stanwick and the high-status goods found there, Cartimandua must have had access to a certain amount of means. She undoubtedly received subsidies from Rome in return for her continued co-operation and as head of the federation of tribes in Brigantia and the owner of large amounts of land, there would be people owing her fealty. She may also have inherited riches from her powerful ancestors. However, in comparison to Prasutagus, the king of the Iceni famed for his prosperity, Cartimandua's fortune may have been relatively modest. The queen received further riches and influence as a reward for her 'treacherous capture' of Caratacus and by this act is said to have provided Claudius with the ultimate finale for his earlier post-conquest triumph (Tacitus, *Histories*, 3.45). This is unlikely, as the emperor celebrated the annexation of Britain eight years before the Catuvellaunian prince was brought to Rome, but Claudius was happy to magnify the significance of such a defeat. The celebrations, designed to heap glory on the emperor, had the dual effect of increasing the reputation of the conquered leader and distracting the people from the political friction in Rome (Berresford Ellis, 1990).

Cartimandua may have removed a dangerous rebel leader from the fight in Britain, but she was certainly not praised by the sources. Michael Grant's translation of Tacitus' *Annals* (1996, 267) talks of Caratacus being 'arrested', but others describe the prince as being 'bound' and handed over to his captors. This treatment would have been an insult for a man of such high standing and would emphasise Cartimandua's wrongdoing in the eyes of the Roman audience. Her continued loyalty to Rome was not seen as a virtue, but an example of her *servitium* (servitude) to the Empire, whilst Caratacus, the enemy of Rome, is praised as a champion of *libertas* (liberty), a favourite theme in Tacitus' work (Braund, 1996, 127-8). Cartimandua was probably a Roman citizen at this time, a status either inherited or granted in return for her allegiance. However, she was still a queen ruling in her own right and that seems to have been enough to merit censure in Tacitus' eyes. No doubt the admiration for the dignity shown by Caratacus in defeat was meant to prove a stark and dramatic contrast to the disapproval of Cartimandua's perfidy. In praising the rebel leader as an opponent, it only emphasises the greatness of the nation who eventually conquered him and then showed clemency. Caratacus had been spared the bloody fate of Vercingetorix (the Gaul who surrendered to Julius Caesar) and other defeated tribal rulers who had been brought to Rome for execution. Caratacus was allowed to remain in exile in Rome with his family. If Cleopatra had lived to be paraded through the streets of the capital, it is unlikely that she would have been shown similar kindness.

FREEDOM FIGHTERS OR FRUSTRATED RULERS?

Most of the rebels against Roman rule in Britain began as allies or consorts of allied monarchs. Caratacus was heir to the Catuvellaunian throne and prior to his father's death had no doubt enjoyed the benefits of Roman friendship. Boudica was married to the rich Prasutagus, a client king and until her territory was annexed in such a brutal fashion by the procurator's men, she too would have reaped the rewards of friendship with the Empire. She may always have opposed her husband's treaty with Rome, but there is no evidence that she expected to succeed him and rule in her own right, as Prasutagus made a Roman will, leaving his kingdom to his two daughters and the Emperor Nero. The action was undoubtedly an attempt at safeguarding some kind of legacy for his family, although he must have known that full annexation was a possibility. Venutius, as we have seen, was initially perfectly happy to support his wife's co-operation with Rome. This changed when she divorced him and later married a member of the royal household, Vellocatus.

Both Boudica and Caratacus have been described as freedom fighters. Princeton University's WordNet defines this as 'a person who takes part in an armed rebellion against the constituted authority (especially in the hope of improving conditions)'. By this standard, both leaders could qualify, in that they wished to improve their own situation, but was their motivation the desire for their people's liberty? Boaz Ganor, a counter-terrorism expert, disagrees with the cliché that 'one man's terrorist is another man's freedom fighter'. He believes the distinction may be drawn by the use of civilian targets to attain political ends (Ganor, 1998, 6) and cites Professor Benzion Netanyahu (1985, 27) to illustrate the point:

> For in contrast to the terrorist, no freedom fighter has ever deliberately attacked innocents. He has never deliberately killed small children, or passers-by in the street, or foreign visitors, or other civilians who happen to reside in the area of conflict or are merely associated ethnically or religiously with the people of that area ... The conclusion we must draw from all this is evident. Far from being a bearer of freedom, the terrorist is the carrier of oppression and enslavement.

Different perspectives will of course produce different labels and the experience of the rebels of ancient Britain is one far removed from our own. If Dio (*Roman History*, 62.7.2) is to be believed, the atrocities perpetrated by Boudica in her attacks on Colchester and London would qualify her as a terrorist by the above definition, since defenceless people, especially women, were targeted.

The Icenian queen certainly had grievances to avenge. In his *Annals*, Tacitus describes how on the death of her husband, the entire friendly territory was annexed and treated as if it had been conquered in battle. The nobles were deprived of their inherited lands, the royal household treated like slaves, Boudica herself was flogged and her two young daughters raped. The kingdom did indeed suffer from this change in leadership, but it seems that the aristocracy bore the brunt of the assault – would the lower classes have considered themselves to be 'free' before this happened? The new conditions may have been tougher for the common people, with the imposition of more financial burdens, more of them taken as slaves and more crops and livestock needed for the Roman Army, but it is not known if Prasutagus had been a benevolent king or if his famed wealth was the result of exploiting his own people.

Modern notions of freedom are often relied upon in reading such accounts, but for the Icenian people, they may have merely exchanged a king for a Roman governor. Slavery was a prominent part of Britain well before the Roman invasion and the island was noted for its human exports (Strabo, 4.5.2). Balsdon (1979) makes the point that 'most of the fine speeches, of course, about liberty outside the empire and servitude inside it were given to princelings and chiefs; and as far as they themselves were concerned, there was a large measure of truth in what they said'. Having been an independent ruler, once the king adopted friendly status, for all of the benefits he may have incurred, he continued to rule only as long as Rome allowed him to. Tacitus gives several examples of such elaborate speeches. He has Boudica describing how she is no longer fighting for her loss of status and riches but for her 'lost freedom' (Tacitus, *Annals*, 14.35) and in the monologue given to the Caledonian, Calgacus, fighting Roman forces in Scotland, Tacitus raises some interesting issues:

> The Brigantes, with only a woman to lead them, burned a Roman colony and stormed a camp; and if success had not tempted them to relax their efforts, they might have cast off the yoke. We, who have never been forced to feel that yoke, shall be fighting to preserve our freedom, and not, like them, merely to avenge past injuries.
>
> *Agricola*, 31

Firstly, he confuses Boudica with Cartimandua and thus the Brigantes with the combined forces of the Iceni and Trinovantes tribes. It has been suggested that this may not have been a mistake and that a female leader of the Brigantes after Cartimandua could have attacked a Roman fort (Allason-Jones, 2005, 9), but it is more likely that this was either an error made in the copying of his work or a mistake made by Tacitus himself. Calgacus's speech suggests that the Icenian rebellion was not really about the loss of liberty that the author's Boudica later bemoans, but more a settling of scores. The freedom fighter in this dramatic scenario is the Caledonian who has never been under the oppression of Rome, implying again that true independence may only be found outside the remit of the Empire. Tacitus echoes this theme in several other passages. Earlier in the *Agricola* he talks about Cogidubnus' loyalty as a friendly king being an example of Rome 'employing even kings to make others slaves' (14) and in the *Annals* he speaks of the Trinovantes tribe joining with Boudica because slavery had not yet cowed them (14.31).

Boudica could have been fighting to free her family and her people from the possibility of further abuses. This brutal treatment was not unique to alien peoples, however, as many prominent Romans and their families had suffered similar fates under the whims of certain emperors and their wives. Rich men were killed so their estates would become forfeit and it is said that the wealthy consul Valerius Asiaticus was condemned because the Empress Messalina coveted his gardens (Tacitus, *Annals*, 11.1). However, Caratacus was not fighting against oppression or for the freedom of his people. He left the Catuvellauni after being defeated in the early days of the invasion and then moved into the west to lead the Welsh tribes against Rome. His tribe may have suffered for his continuous resistance and his brother's initial stand against the Empire. After both leaders were gone from their native territory, the Catuvellauni could also have been subjected to reprisals from the neighbouring lands conquered by the princes' earlier expansionist policies after Cunobelin's death. Unfortunately, a pattern emerges – after defeat, Caratacus would move on to the next opportunity, leaving the people who had supported him to deal with the consequences of his actions. His own tribe were abandoned once they could not or did not aid him in rebellion and the Silures and Ordovices were left with his own family to face the invading forces of Rome. The Brigantes were only saved from being added to this list of casualties by the intervention of their queen.

Caratacus was plainly fighting for freedom – the freedom to rule as he saw fit. For the people he coerced into obedience in expanding his kingdom and the leaders whose birthright he usurped in taking command of the Welsh tribes, he could have been seen as a symbol of oppression and not liberty. In the speech given to him by Tacitus at the triumph in Rome, the rebel leader talks of how things could have been if he had come before the emperor as a friend and ally. The likelihood is that if Caratacus or his brother had been allowed to succeed their father on the Catuvellaunian throne, then the prince would not have turned rebel and would have been just another friendly monarch (as his brother may have later become). He fought against Rome not to better the prospects of his people, but because his own birthright had been taken away: 'I had horses, men, arms, wealth. Are you surprised I am sorry to lose them? If you want to rule the world, does it follow that everyone else welcomes enslavement?' (Tacitus, *Annals*, 12.37). Many people have fought bravely for such reasons – there is nothing wrong with wanting to protect their position and lands and to avenge wrongs done to themselves and their families. In denying their role as freedom fighters, it is mainly correcting a misconception. They started out as beneficiaries of their relatives' alliances with Rome, but both Boudica and Caratacus could have disagreed with these policies and simply followed their own inclinations once their respective husband and father were no longer in control. Many great leaders have not been acting from purely selfless motives – it does not lessen their achievements to find out that they were not perfect. The British have always supported the underdog and although Boudica and Caratacus did not ultimately succeed against Rome, they put up a good fight. It is just another example of the situation having shades of grey instead of the extremes of gleaming white or midnight black.

Popular media has not helped our view of the ancient concept of freedom. Watching the film *Braveheart* (1995) and hearing the immortal line: 'Tell our enemies that they may take our lives, but they'll never take our freedom!' makes most of us want to reach for the nearest sharp object in defending our sofa. Unfortunately, like the chained galley slaves rowing the Roman warships in *Ben-Hur* (1959), it has no basis in historical fact (James, 2001, 35-6). The people in thirteenth- and fourteenth-century Scotland had little more liberty than their ancient British cousins did and free citizens and professional seamen were often in charge of the oars in the Roman fleet. However, as with Tacitus and his emotive speeches, these dramatic exaggerations and imaginings make for great viewing.

THE 'FIRST' BRIGANTIAN REBELLION

Venutius is described as 'the best strategist' since Caratacus was captured (Tacitus, *Annals*, 12.40), but the Romans did not tend to admire the Britons for their military planning. Any praise for the natives in battle seems to be reserved for their bravery in being willing to die rather than submit to Roman authority. Far from being known for their tactical long-term preparations, the 'barbarians' were thought to be impetuous and undisciplined (Balsdon, 1979). For Venutius to be mentioned in this fashion there must have been some evidence of particular aptitude in this area. It could also be another example of the sources heaping praise on someone who later fought against Rome, making him out to be a worthy opponent, but that does not mean that the tribute was undeserved. As the earlier reference to the Brigantian in the *Annals* is lost to us now, we can only surmise what was discussed. He could have spent some time with the Roman Army and acquired some knowledge of military matters there, or he may even have advised Ostorius Scapula or another Roman leader from a native point of view. Tacitus talks of Venutius having long-standing loyalty and mentions that he was defended by Roman arms whilst married to the tribal queen. De la Bédoyère interprets this to mean that Venutius may have been threatened by the Brigantian rebels in AD 47 and that he had been involved in the surrender of Caratacus, hoping to gain more influence and replace him as the first among the British chieftains (2003, 78). This would not have been possible whilst he remained as Cartimandua's consort, but the trouble that began to brew in the royal household is said to have started sometime after the capture of Caratacus. As the queen's consort, it is entirely possible that he was content to support her alliance with the Empire until their relationship became troubled and then any ambitions he may have had could have surfaced. If Venutius had been leader of his own tribe prior to their marriage, he would have been used to the respect of his people. As Cartimandua's husband, the Brigantes would still have seen him as king, but the Romans would have looked down on any man ruled by his wife:

> If we had, each one of us, made it a rule to uphold the rights and authority of the husband in our own households we should not now have this trouble with the whole body of our women. As things are now our liberty of action, which has been checked and rendered powerless by female despotism at home, is actually crushed and trampled on here in the Forum ... Our ancestors would have no woman transact even private business except through her guardian, they placed them under the tutelage of parents or brothers or husbands. We suffer them now to dabble in politics and mix themselves up with the business of the Forum and public debates and election contests ... Call to mind all the regulations respecting women by which our ancestors curbed their licence and made them obedient to their husbands, and yet in spite of all those restrictions you can scarcely hold them in. If you allow them to pull away these restraints and wrench them out one after another, and finally put themselves on an equality with their husbands, do you imagine that you will be able to tolerate them? From the moment that they become your fellows they will become your masters.
>
> Livy, *The History of Rome*, 34.2-3

The six-year period following Caratacus's arrest saw major changes in both Britain and Rome. Ostorius Scapula died in AD 52 and was replaced as governor by Didius Gallus. Two years later, the Emperor Claudius was murdered. The sources suggest that his wife, Agrippina, poisoned him to make way for her son Nero's rise to power (Suetonius, *Claudius*, 44; Tacitus, *Annals*, 12.66-7). In the midst of these shifts in command, Venutius and Cartimandua divorced. It is not known whether a consort could divorce a tribal ruler, but it may be assumed that the queen decided to end their marriage as she is seen as the target for the hostilities that followed. It is possible to speculate on the cause of this break-up. Theirs could have been a dynastic union, as political alliances were common in many royal circles. With ancestry and lineage being of such importance to many ancient cultures, the divorce could have occurred because of the absence of heirs, as no mention is ever made of Cartimandua having children. In Rome, an unproductive marriage could easily be dissolved without stigma (D'Ambra, 2007, 46) and divorce was no doubt possible in ancient Britain.

This, however, would assume that the queen suspected or even knew that she could conceive a child with someone else and there is no evidence that adultery was the cause of the separation. Tacitus says that Venutius showed enmity towards his wife and then Rome after the divorce, but tensions may have been brewing before the split. If he wished to take a greater share in power or had decided not to continue his loyalty to the Empire, Cartimandua may have decided that it would be wise to distance herself from a relationship that may cause her trouble, especially if her husband was popular with the people. His commitment to the Roman cause cannot have been deeply felt, for he was willing to discard it after a quarrel with his wife. Aldhouse-Green (2006, 127) makes the point that 'he appears to have been wooed by the vicarious power, status and Roman friendship emanating from his wife, but underneath he chafed both at his own inferior rank and at Cartimandua's position as the real authority'.

Whatever the cause of the royal estrangement, it initially led to fighting amongst the Brigantes. The various factions within the tribal alliance will have no doubt chosen sides and this in-fighting led to the seizure of Venutius' brother and other relations. This seems a very drastic step to take if all that had happened was a divorce. Cartimandua's in-laws could have been a powerful family who headed one of the tribes (possibly the Carvetii) in the Brigantian federation. If they had threatened to support Venutius in rallying forces against Cartimandua, such a risk to her position would have to be neutralised, which would explain their imprisonment. However, far from being the end of the matter, the conflict escalated to include the invasion of the kingdom by a strong external force. Venutius had managed to raise support outside of the tribe, but it seems unlikely that the dissolution of the royal marriage alone would have caused such repercussions. Tacitus says that Cartimandua's enemies invaded her kingdom as they were 'infuriated and goaded by fears of humiliating feminine rule' (Tacitus, *Annals*, 12.40). The fact that external forces attacked the kingdom to avoid such a consequence suggests a fear that Cartimandua would expand her territory. Yet it seems unlikely that the queen would wish to extend her already vast realm, especially as she was having trouble keeping control of the areas she did rule. As it has already been established that the Britons were accustomed to female leadership, the tone of this comment says more about the Roman author's attitude to female rulers than the motive for conflict. A more likely interpretation is that Venutius and his warriors invaded the realm in an attempt to rescue the hostages.

Once again, Cartimandua was able to rely on Roman aid. The new governor may have been monitoring the situation once the internal fighting began, as he is said to have anticipated the need for military support and sent auxiliary troops into Brigantia. Resistance must have been sustained, since several skirmishes occurred, but a clear victory was not achieved until the legion commanded by Caesius Nasica (possibly the IX *Hispana*) finally met with success. Didius Gallus had had a full career by the time he took the post as governor. It is possible that he wished to further his fortunes and retire on the rich pickings of victories in Britain. If so, he will have been disappointed. Tacitus is dismissive of his conduct in Brigantia, though there is a suggestion that such criticism was based on a personal dislike of the man derived from the prejudice of others (Webster, 1993a, 87-8).

The financial pros and cons of invading Britain had long been debated in Rome. In the early years of Nero's reign, the teenage emperor was advised by the cautious wisdom of the philosopher, Seneca and the commander of the Praetorian Guard, Burrus. The costs of occupation and maintaining a military presence were believed to be more than offset by the gains in income that would come from the exploitation of the island's resources. However, the province did not prove to be an untapped store of riches and with the constant threat from restless tribes, it must often have seemed literally more trouble than it was worth. Decisions about Britain were originally postponed for further consideration, but Nero is said to have contemplated withdrawing his legions from Britain, only deciding not to do so as such an action may have tarnished the memory of his step-father, Claudius' 'triumph' there (Suetonius, *Nero*, 18). However, by AD 57, Nero resolved to subdue the Welsh tribes and Didius Gallus was recalled from the province to be replaced by Veranius Nepos. This seasoned soldier reversed his predecessor's policy of maintaining existing borders and began military operations against the troublesome Silures, but died within a year.

With his invasion defeated, Venutius must have fled to his own people. There is no evidence to suggest that he managed to rescue his relatives and so the situation between the estranged couple must still have been fraught. Richmond (1954, 50) and others have proposed a reconciliation between the royal couple, but given the violence of their initial separation, such a possibility seems highly improbable. Rome would have been anxious to maintain the security of the Brigantian frontier, but it is unlikely that they would appreciate the restoration to power of a man confirmed as a dangerous rebel. Like any concerned 'parent', they would want their 'daughter' to distance herself from a troublesome partner. Cartimandua would have been in a difficult situation – she would have wanted to address the concerns of her Roman allies and was surely longing for peace in her kingdom herself. However, if she allowed Roman troops to go after Venutius, she would again be risking further rifts within the tribe, for her ex-husband had shown his popularity with at least some of the people. If there were also personal reasons for the split, she would have had no desire to have him under the same roof again. Thus, a compromise could have been reached. If Venutius returned to his native tribe and pledged to cause no further trouble, Cartimandua may have averted further Roman reprisals for his attack. It is quite possible that she would not trust any assurances and so may have kept his relatives as collateral. As the unsuccessful party, he would have had no choice but to comply and in doing so, lived to plot and fight another day. As such, an uneasy peace would have been established to mutual benefit.

CAUSES OF TENSION IN THE SOUTH-EAST

As the embers of the Brigantian rebellion began to cool, elsewhere in Britain resentment began to smoulder. During the AD 50s, a colony was established at Colchester (Camulodunum). Here, retired Roman soldiers would be given a piece of land and encouraged to settle with their dependants in the town. This was common practice in the administration of the Empire. Unfortunately, the land distributed to these ex-soldiers was confiscated from the existing tribal owners – in this case, members of the Trinovantes tribe. Hingley and Unwin (2005, 23-4) describe how the tribal aristocracy were left in possession of their lands, presumably to ensure their co-operation in the establishment of the settlement. Disgruntled natives, dispossessed of their homes and ancestral lands, had more grievances to report. The tribe may initially have welcomed the Roman advance as it delivered them from Catuvellaunian aggression, but such feelings were short-lived. The settlers were said to have taken liberties with the local people and the construction of a temple to the now divine Claudius, built with local funds, was a focus for resentment. Built on the site of an abandoned fort, the colony would have been supervised by the veteran inhabitants, but as construction occurred no new defences were erected. Such complacent behaviour shows not only a lack of foresight, but also a want of appreciation of the tensions in the territory. It could be assumed that ex-military men would have been used to protecting themselves in a much better fashion, but it was not the only occasion when the Romans failed to safeguard an occupied area. The assumption, that once initially conquered any tribal resistance would not be contemplated, was a dangerous one.

Some time around AD 60-1, the neighbouring Iceni lost their king, Prasutagus, and his death sparked the conflict that was to overwhelm the province. As previously mentioned, the client ruler had left a will naming his two young daughters and the Emperor Nero as 'co-heirs'. Braund (1984a, 144) makes the interesting point that the intended division of the royal estate is not known – Prasutagus could have desired one of the princesses to succeed to his throne, but he could equally have bequeathed the kingdom to Nero and left legacies to his daughters. Rome had invested heavily in Britain. Claudius was said to have given substantial sums to leading British chieftains – opinion is divided as to the nature of the transaction, with some believing the amounts to be gifts and others believing them to be loans. In the hope of gaining a decent rate of interest, the emperor's advisor, Seneca had personal commitments of 40 million *sesterces* in the region. Holland (2000, 129) believes that in his privileged position in government, Nero's mentor would have known that the entire Icenian kingdom was going to be annexed by the Empire. The treaty with the client monarch had expired on his death and with the existence of a will or not, the estate of the famously wealthy king was considered fair game. To compound the problem, it had been decided that the monies advanced by Claudius had to be reimbursed and Seneca demanded the repayment of his hefty loan all at once (Dio, *Roman History*, 62.2.1) before the Imperial Procurator, Decianus Catus could seize any Icenian assets. The unfortunate Iceni were subjected to a range of violence and insults as their territory was plundered: the princesses were raped, the queen flogged, the nobility dispossessed of their estates and the kingdom treated like the spoils of war (Tacitus, *Annals*, 14.31). Tacitus does not seem to fault the justification to annex the Icenian kingdom, but he does attack the violent manner in which it was carried out. In this explosion of brutality, the new governor, Suetonius Paulinus was where any competent leader would be – at the other end of the country.

THE DRUIDS

Pagan beliefs are linked very closely with a reverence for the living world and the spirits that inhabit natural things. The sun, moon, fire, water, earth and air are all seen as central to the circle of life and death, inherent in the changing seasons. Druids in antiquity are portrayed as a powerful and highly organised priesthood, who directed tribal ritual, reading the omens and signs from the gods and studying the stars and the heavens among their many functions. Ellison (2005) believes that Druids were unlikely to be involved in the personal religion of the tribe, as each household would have propitiated their own local spirits. In addition to holding ceremonies in the sacred groves (*nemetons*) where oak trees and mistletoe were central to their rites, Druids seemed to perform other secular duties. They are credited with political and inter-tribal influence, advising the nobility, educating the elite youth in the oral tradition and acting as the repository for the tribe's history, ancestral stories and wisdom. What we do know of this religious order comes down to us from ancient Greek and Roman sources, with some early Welsh and Irish documents also mentioning their existence. Most often cited is Julius Caesar's *Gallic War*, as he seemed fascinated by this mystical group, but although many of his observations are said to derive from his subordinates and the stoic philosopher, Posidonius (Mackillop, 2006, 26), Caesar was acquainted with the Gallic Aeduan, Diviciacus, who was a Druid himself. Much of the literature focuses on the Druids of Gaul, but others do recognise that the order was present in Britain (Pliny, *The Natural History*, 30.4.3).

Roman and British religious beliefs centring on a pantheon of gods, superstition and ritual, can seem alien to a modern Christian audience. However, as Balsdon (1979) points out, many pagans would find the belief in one god, crucified in the form of a man, physically resurrected to his body after death and preaching the benefits of not avenging any wrongs done to them, extraordinary. As we have seen, Romans away from their home frequently incorporated the native gods into their worship. Both visitor and native had a high regard for the importance of omens, dreams and the necessity of waiting for auspicious times to act, and many deities were propitiated with animal sacrifices. Yet many emperors forbade the practice of Druidism – the reason given by many of the sources was the rite of human sacrifice. It seems strange that a people who buried erring Vestal Virgins alive, watched animals devouring humans in the arena and had such a fondness for gladiatorial fights to the death, would be miffed at the idea of the odd barbarian killing one of their own. So was there another reason that the Druids were considered dangerous? Hingley and Unwin (2005, 17) propose that rather than being dismayed at the concept of ritual murder, the Romans knew the Druids to be a focus for acts of resistance. We have already examined Webster's idea of the Druids as a uniting force, which could have used their influence to smooth Caratacus' passage into Wales. Frere (1987) suggests that opposition to Cartimandua's alliance with Rome in AD 47 may have been encouraged by the Druid stronghold in Anglesey, who feared their isolation from any sources of support in Brigantia. Mixing politics and religion could have been the key to Roman objection as anyone supporting rebels and inciting resistance would be classed as an enemy. If the theory of Druidic control of the gold route from Ireland is at all plausible, then the priesthood could have been seen as an economic threat, as well as a political one (Trow, 2003, 96). Any group with power over the people would be seen as dangerous by a military power determined to conquer territory and enforce the submission of its inhabitants.

It has been proposed that the influence of the Druids declined at some time before the conquest of Britain. Creighton (1995, 297, 300) discusses their changing role in Iron Age society as the priestly function of the order conflicted with the interests of the new political structures. With the new forms of kingship appearing in the south-eastern dynasties, the structure of power and influence in political and religious contexts began to evolve in a way that may not have been compatible with the old ways. Webster (1999) agrees with Creighton's concept of the declining fortunes of the Druids in Britain, but she questions the timing of such a deterioration, believing the catalyst to be the conquest itself. She suggests that the association of the Druids with remote and private places could be an indication that the order had emerged as an 'underground movement', whose interests were incompatible with those of Rome. However much the power of the Druids had been weakened, they were still considered to be enough of a threat for the governor, Suetonius Paulinus to advance on their stronghold in Anglesey (Mona) in AD 60.

Nero had appointed a man experienced in mountain warfare – a quality that would be well tested in finishing the conquest of the rebellious Welsh tribes and extending Rome's occupied territory in the west. The island of Anglesey must have seemed like a symbol of resistance to the Romans. Its population swollen by refugees from campaigns against the Empire, it was the site of the Ordovician and Silurian granaries and the final sanctuary of the Druids. Suetonius Paulinus was an ambitious man and the idea of destroying such an enemy stronghold must have been appealing. The troops were forced to cross the Menai Straits in the face of cursing Druids and fanatical women (Tacitus, *Annals*, 14.30), knowing that the cornered Britons would fight to the death. Roman victory saw the sacred groves destroyed and the population slain. It must have been a very satisfying outcome for Suetonius Paulinus, until he realised that in leaving to campaign in Wales, he had exposed his rear to attack. Making the fatal error of assuming that the south-eastern territories were secure, he was now faced with the knowledge that his forces were too divided to provide an adequate defence.

LINDOW MAN

In August 1984, workers at Lindow Moss Farm in Cheshire discovered the body of a man, preserved in the peat (Fig. 9). Nothing below his waist

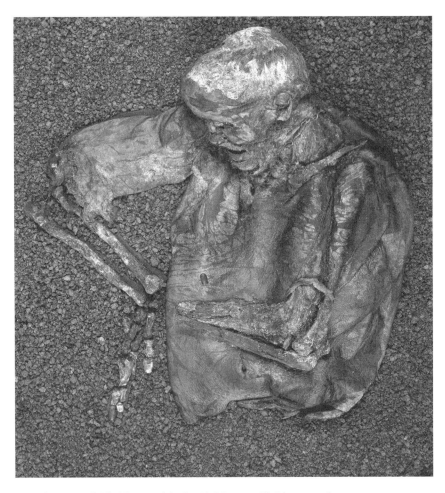

9 Lindow Man © *The Trustees of the British Museum. All rights reserved*

was found originally as it is believed that the excavating equipment had cut him in half, but parts of his legs and buttocks were later uncovered. Radiocarbon dating was inconclusive at first, but recent estimates place the death of the man between AD 20 and AD 90 (British Museum). 'Pete Marsh', as he was affectionately christened, was a contemporary of Cartimandua and his body was actually found in what was once Brigantian territory. The damp environment of the bog led to extraordinary levels of preservation so that the man's skin, his hair and most of his internal organs survived in the peat. Lindow II or Lindow Man (to give him his official title) was in his mid twenties when he died. Apart from a bad case of parasitic worms and a touch of arthritis in his back, he was in reasonably good health and stood around 5ft 6in tall. Pete was thought not to have done any recent manual labour as his nails were well manicured. He had healthy teeth and his beard had been groomed using shears rather than a single blade – all the evidence points towards him being of high status and having had a privileged life.

Found naked, wearing only an armband of fox fur, it has been suggested that Pete may have been wearing some form of body paint or woad. Morgan and Morgan (2004) explain that an excess of copper, aluminium, titanium and zinc were found in an analysis of the man's skin. They believe that this could have been caused by drinking water from the mineral veins of local Alderley Edge, eating foods grown in soils with a high copper content or wearing some copper-based pigment painted onto his skin. The copper ore malachite was mined on the Edge, so if this had been used his body would have been stained green, rather than the famous blue associated with ancient British warriors that woad produces. The question of whether Lindow Man was painted with woad or another substance remains open. The amount of copper found on his skin was not enough to suggest a definite answer and although Caesar mentioned all Britons dyeing themselves with some sort of blue colouring (*Gallic War*, 5.14), there is scant evidence for the tradition of woad-staining as a widespread practice (Turner & Scaife, 1995). It could be that in a time of changing concepts of identity, body painting was a way of showing resistance against the 'Roman' way, or it could have been reserved for special occasions: to enhance the power of the warrior in battle or to mark a rite of passage (Carr, 2005, 284-5).

If Lindow Man's body was painted in such a way, the manner of his death could explain why. Pete died a 'threefold death', when any one of the actions would have been enough to end his life. Struck twice on the back of the head, possibly when kneeling, with blows so strong that one of his teeth cracked and fragments of his skull became embedded in his brain, he also received a heavy blow to his back that fractured one of his ribs. A garrotte made of animal gut was then used to strangle him and break his neck – the ligature was found still attached to his throat when the body was discovered. He was probably already dead at this point but just to make sure, his throat was cut, the jugular vein sliced with a sharp blade. Pete was then placed face down in the water of the bog. The triple death was thought to be evidence of a ritual killing, as three was a number which held significance in the ancient pagan world and the 'three deaths' could have been a sacrifice to three separate gods or even to each aspect of a triple-god.

Other factors have contributed to the idea that the man died as part of a religious rite. The contents of Lindow Man's stomach revealed that shortly before he died, he had consumed some blackened grains. Mistletoe pollen was also found in his gut. It does not seem like much of a last meal, but one apparently highly significant to his ultimate fate. Burnt bread was a way of choosing a victim to be sacrificed in certain pagan festivals, especially at the spring rite of Beltane and mistletoe was a plant especially revered by the Druids (Brothwell, 1986). By dying in such a fashion, having drunk the pollen of a potent and sacred plant, and being buried with the band of fox fur, Lindow Man could have been conferring potency and prosperity on his people (Stead *et al*, 1986) and appeasing their gods. Another possibility is that the sacrifice was used for divinatory purposes and that in the throes of death, the victim gave some sign that could be interpreted by the Druids to show the best course of action to take (Turner & Scaife, 1995).

Being buried in the watery bog could also be of ritual significance. The ancient Britons believed that such places were gateways between the worlds and precious objects were commonly deposited thus. To make such offerings sacred, they were 'removed' from the human world – in the case of a weapon or other material object, it would be badly damaged, rendering it useless in a practical sense; for an animal or a human offering, they would be slaughtered in order to enter the realm of the divine (Green, 2001). Although he was found in Brigantian territory, he may not have been a native of the tribe. His high status could have been as leader of his people or as a Druid. It could be that like the Vestal Virgins in Rome, the behaviour of the tribal religious figure reflected on the fortunes of the community. In volunteering or being chosen to die in such a fashion, it would suggest that a great misfortune had befallen the people, that needed the sacrifice of something important, and a man or woman of influence could have been the tribe's most precious offering (Morgan & Morgan, 2004). Despite the constant references to such barbaric practices from Roman authors, a human sacrifice was probably a very rare occurrence, considered necessary in response to a terrible ill or at a time when the people believed their gods to be very displeased. Famine or war could necessitate such a ritual and Lindow Man died in very uncertain times. If he had been a Druid, the slaughter of his people at Mona could indicate their deities' disfavour and as the land had been devastated by conquest, rebellion and the aftermath of such upheaval, the gods needed to be propitiated.

The ancient pagans were thought to be unafraid of dying, as they believed that their soul would go on to the Otherworld – if Lindow Man was painted in woad, this could have been the rite of passage that he was prepared for. This belief in the continuity of life could explain the many acts of bravery in battle for which the ancient Britons were famous. In death they were often equipped for the pleasures of fighting, feasting and even riding in their next life too, as their weapons and sometimes even their chariot were buried with them. This was not an exclusively male privilege as the Iron Age inhumation found at Wetwang Slack in Yorkshire shows – here a young woman was buried with her chariot, a couple of pig joints and other grave goods around 300 BC.

THE BOUDICAN REVOLT

On the back of the outrages committed against their people, the seizure of ancestral lands and weapons, and the demands for huge sums of money, the Iceni and Trinovantes tribes, who had both enjoyed peaceful alliances with the Empire in the past, were provoked to join together in rebellion against Rome. Tacitus says that the entire island rose up behind Boudica (*Agricola*, 16), but the rebellion may have had a very different outcome if that were true. England was not a united country.

Carr (2005, 282-3) cites Webster's theory of 'creolization' (2001) in examining the changing identity of a person living in post-conquest Britain – the static terms 'native' and 'Roman' are abandoned in favour of a more fluid approach to such hybrid cultures. In its historical context, the term 'creole' was used to describe people born in the colonies to set them apart from the European-born upper-class immigrants. Creolization, in a general sense, can be seen as 'all kinds of cross-fertilization that takes place between different cultures when they interact' (Cohen, 2007). Far from being the replacement of one way of life with another, such interaction would result in each culture selecting and adapting certain elements of the new society, merging them with their own to create a new mixed tradition. Just as a larger company keeps certain essential elements of the smaller firm it takes over, and then introduces new adaptations and innovations developed around this sound base, so the cultures of Rome and Britain were merged across a sliding scale. Those members of the native nobility anxious to show their status may have adopted more of the occupier's ways than those in the northern highland farming communities largely unaffected in the short term by the new regime.

Davies (1999, 14) describes the various communities living in Iron Age Britain as 'neither unified nor uniform'. Different regions had their own type of settlements, their own traditions and material culture and their own inter-tribal relationships, and things were constantly shifting. The native groupings we know about from the Roman authors could have been changed, created or merged for administrative or political convenience and may have had little or no resemblance to pre-existing tribal territories. Client relationships with the Empire could have resulted in changing boundaries, with a favoured ruler being given control of a 'kingdom' comprising several tribal groupings. Those ambitious British nobles who were governed mainly by their own interests may have been criticised by the people they ruled, but they cannot be said to have been unpatriotic as there was no nation to which they could have shown loyalty. The joining of the Iceni and their neighbours in revolt was an example of groups coming together against a shared perceived threat – ignoring their tribal differences, they united under a common hatred provoked by a more alien Other (James, 1999, 103).

Dyson (1975) describes how the native revolt is a feature of any society dealing with imperialism – ancient rebellions bear many of the same features as uprisings against modern colonial society. He makes the interesting point that these revolts often arise at a time when the empire believes the troubles of conquest to be over. Ignoring the tensions arising from conflicts between the new settlers and the natives, the difficulties of adjusting to a new financial and administrative system, and the invariable abuses that any invasion will bring, the new governors are often shocked and surprised by the violence and extent of the native objection.

In AD 60 Suetonius Paulinus was away campaigning in Wales. The Iceni were still reeling from their treatment at the hands of the procurator's men and Trinovantian hostility to the settlers on their native land simmered below the surface. It is not a huge leap for us to imagine that an uprising would break out and yet it did not occur to the Romans.

Boudica was the widowed queen of the Iceni, who may have had no expectations of ruling her people in her own right – the neighbouring tribes owed her no fealty and yet they responded to her call to arms. She could have been a very persuasive leader as Caratacus was thought to be, but unlike her Catuvellaunian contemporary, she had no experience of heading an army (that we know of). There has been some suggestion that Boudica may have had some religious status as well as being the leader of her people, which is perhaps what drew the tribes to follow her into battle, but we shall come back to this idea shortly.

The Romans could well have expected some sort of backlash after the violence against Boudica and her household, but because there was no immediate response, the Imperial forces may have been lulled into a false sense of security. The Britons were thought to be incapable of longer-term planning – maybe their experiences in rebellion so far had taught them to wait and use caution instead of reacting immediately in anger. Giving the outward appearance of a defeated people, the rebels must have been secretly re-arming themselves and attempting to form alliances with others sympathetic to their cause. Meetings between the tribal groups would have been held in secret and for old rivalries to be forgotten, there must have been some skilled diplomatic negotiation. Who better to facilitate such communication than a group revered by all in a religious capacity? Waite (2007, 144) suggests that the influential Druid order could have acted as impartial messengers, as mediators between the tribes smoothing any ruffled feathers and as advisors with the knowledge of who to approach for support. They could have been hoping that in helping to bring the tribes together in the south-east and promoting rebellion, an uprising would prove a distraction to the governor's forces. In turning to protect his rear as Scapula had done, Suetonius Paulinus may have abandoned the attack on Mona and the refugees could have been spared. Unfortunately, events did not turn out that way.

The governor must have known that the entire Icenian kingdom was going to be absorbed into the Empire by force and although he may not have realised the brutal steps that Decianus Catus and his men would take in subduing the population, he must have expected some objection. It is possible that after their uprising was defeated in AD 47, the Romans believed the Iceni to be sensible of the consequences of resisting the Empire, and that Suetonius Paulinus expected the tribal opposition, if any, to be on a small scale and able to be managed by those literally 'holding the fort'. With centuries of image reinforcement portraying Rome as the invincible war machine, it seems almost unfathomable that a seasoned commander would make the classic blunder of not guarding his flank, but we know that as with most propaganda, this image was not totally correct. Rome had a full-time professional army of soldiers trained in discipline and strategy, led by men with experience of many campaigns. However, they were only human and Suetonius Paulinus clearly misjudged the situation, paying the price for making assumptions. If only they had had management seminars in those days, he would have known that to assume makes an 'ass' of 'u' and 'me'.

Colchester seems to have been a trophy of conquest as each invading force had taken it as their capital – first, the Catuvellauni, who under Cunobelin moved their tribal base there after subduing the Trinovantes, and later the Romans, after Claudius chose it as his administrative centre. In AD 60, the colony there was undefended. The site of the hated Temple of Claudius and the home of the retired soldiers who had taken so much from the tribal natives, it seems a logical choice for the first target of the Boudican rebels. It could even have been a condition of Trinovantian involvement that the colony was attacked and destroyed. Once the rebels had fully decided upon their plans, they would have had to act quickly as any mistakes could have meant a very swift end to all their hopes of victory. Strategically, the absence of the governor and his troops was a distinct advantage and one that would not last forever.

As the rebels descended on the town, they brought their woman and children with them, only too aware of the dangers of leaving them at home to face Roman reprisals. With their families close, Boudica's forces could see what they were fighting for. If the literary devices Tacitus was so fond of are to believed, then there were portents of doom aplenty, with the statue of Victory falling down on its front as if running from the oncoming danger, the sea turning red, disembodied voices yelling and shrieking and a ghostly ruined settlement seen at the mouth of the Thames (Tacitus, *Annals*, 14.32). A Roman audience reading such descriptions would have been well aware of what was coming next – you can just imagine them shouting 'They're behind you' into their papyrus manuscripts. However, the townspeople must have had some warning of the impending attack as they sent to London (Londinium) to ask Decianus Catus for reinforcements. He sent 200 inadequately armed men, before eventually escaping to Gaul, leaving the people of the province to reap the consequences of his actions.

It is possible that Boudican agents misled the colonists that defences were not necessary as legionary protection would soon arrive, or it could just be that in the general mood of optimism and complacency the settlers did not believe that they would be seriously attacked, as the women, children and elderly were not evacuated from the town. Colchester was devastated – buildings were destroyed, including the detested Claudian temple where the inhabitants fled and barricaded themselves in, waiting for a legionary rescue that was never to arrive. The temple was burned around them and the remaining population slaughtered. The Iceni must have felt the favour of their goddess of victory, Andraste. In triumph, the Boudican hordes burned and looted, the blood of the hated settlers spilled in avenging their many grievances. No prisoners were taken and no mercy was shown. Petillius Cerealis, commander of the IX *Hispana* marched south with a detachment of his legion. They were ambushed and the entire force of experienced soldiers was killed, with a few cavalry and their legate fleeing back to their fort.

On hearing the news of the destruction of Colchester, Suetonius Paulinus hastened south with a detachment of cavalry and made for London, leaving his legions to follow behind. Arriving there before Boudica and realising that it could not be defended, the governor abandoned the town to its fate, taking with him only those who could keep up with the pace, and went to rejoin his army on the long march from Wales. Boudica's forces had been occupied with the defeat of the Legion IX *Hispana* and, as news of her victory spread, followers no doubt flocked to her banner. Agreement between the tribes would have to be reached on the next point of attack and with their families and children in tow, progress south would have been slow. London was another undefended settlement – as a centre of commerce, the wealth of some of the inhabitants would have made it a profitable target. The rebels laid waste to the trading centre and the people who had not fled shared the fate of the Colchester colonists. Tacitus does not dwell on the killings, but Dio goes all out in describing the ferocity of the assault. Apparently, there were naked impalings, severed breasts and all manner of savage practices enacted (Dio, *Roman History*, 62.7.1-3). Whether invented, exaggerated or based on an actual event, the fate of both towns was no doubt unpleasant. 'Barbarians' are often credited with such atrocities, but the Roman Army was also known to have committed many unspeakable acts. Although once a client kingdom, the Iceni and their neighbours were now attacking anything that stood for Roman rule – her settlers, her commerce and her allies.

St Albans (Verulamium) was home to the Catuvellauni, Caratacus' tribe. Their past expansionist policies would have meant that the Trinovantes in Boudica's army would be keen to settle old scores. However, in attacking this Roman town with its bathhouse and shops selling high-status and imported goods, the rebels were obliterating the hated symbols of Imperial rule and showing their feelings about those individuals who had embraced the invaders' culture and way of life. As wife to a client monarch, Boudica may have once been on such a path herself, but she was firmly untying her colours from that mast in destroying all symbols of her former life. Unlike Colchester and London, St Albans was not totally obliterated, nor all its inhabitants slaughtered. Some parts of the town escaped the fires and selected surrounding farmsteads were left untouched. It has been suggested that these fortunate homes were owned by local natives who, as such, had nothing to fear from the rebels hell-bent on attacking everything Roman. It may also be that the property and dwellings were spared in return for the support of the Catuvellaunian nobles and their followers (Waite, 2007, 125).

It is possible that some of Boudica's forces had served in the Roman Army as auxiliaries and so may have been familiar with the enemy's tactics and military strategies. History has shown that Rome's military expertise had been used against her more than once. Venutius may have spent some time with Imperial forces and there were incidents where former Roman soldiers led rebellions against Rome. Civilis, a Batavian tribal chief who had served as an auxiliary, took advantage of the political uncertainty in Rome in AD 69 and led the German tribes against the Empire after being falsely accused of treason. Spartacus, the leader of the slave uprising against Rome known as the Third Servile War (73-71 BC), was also once an auxiliary. Appian describes him as 'a Thracian by birth, who had once served as a soldier with the Romans, but had since been a prisoner and sold for a gladiator' (*The Civil Wars*, 1.116). This 'gladiator war' had many similarities with the Boudican Revolt. The rebels easily killed the first force sent against them under an inexperienced praetor, Claudius Glaber, as the Romans had not fortified their camp or posted adequate sentries, underestimating the threat from a group of escaped slaves. In the same way that Boudica's followers grew after her first successes, Spartacus attracted many runaway slaves and their families. He too had women, children and the elderly following him into battle. With such large numbers to control, both Boudica and the ex-gladiator had to persuade their people away from pillaging and keep them moving towards their next target. Spartacus wanted to get his army out of Italy and back to their homes, but a deal with Cilician pirates fell through and he was forced to continue fighting against Rome until the combined forces of Crassus and Pompey ended the rebels' fight for their liberty. As his army was comprised of slaves, theirs was a literal fight for freedom, but they also took the opportunity to avenge wrongs done to them by their Roman masters.

Whilst making his way to rejoin his legions, Suetonius Paulinus would have evaluated the troops at his disposal. Legion IX *Hispana* under Petillius Cerealis had been badly hit by Boudica's ambush and the acting commander of Legion II *Augusta* in Exeter, Poenius Postumus, had disobeyed orders and refused to send his forces to join the governor in London. Thus, the whole of Legion XIV *Gemina*, part of Legion XX *Valeria* and whatever auxiliaries he could summon from other bases, formed the basis of Suetonius Paulinus' force, estimated at around 10,000 men (Sealey, 2004, 38). Even if the 230,000 said to have made up Boudican numbers was exaggerated, the Romans would still have been greatly outnumbered. If the tribal queen had decided to play to her warriors' strengths and wage a guerrilla campaign, using their knowledge of the surrounding countryside to conduct surprise attacks and ambushes on the weary Roman forces, it would have been impossible for the governor to co-ordinate an organised defence. As had been shown by the defeat of the Ninth Legion and the success of Caratacus' forces in Wales, Roman strength depended on a pitched battle to gain the advantage. Unfortunately, this was where the mistake was made as Boudica resolved to pursue the Roman Army, allowing Suetonius Paulinus to choose his own ground. His prayers had been answered – his rear was protected by a wood and the only approach from the front was through a narrow valley, countering the rebel advantage of superior numbers (Fig. 10).

Boudica has been criticised for allowing the Romans to have their head-on fight. She is thought to have been over-confident, believing that her massive forces could succeed on the back of their earlier victories. However, it is worth considering the alternatives. The tribal army was huge – it would have taken a massive effort to support them and keep morale going. If she did not move towards another target, she risked losing troops who may drift off back to their homes in periods of inactivity. Boudica had to maintain her

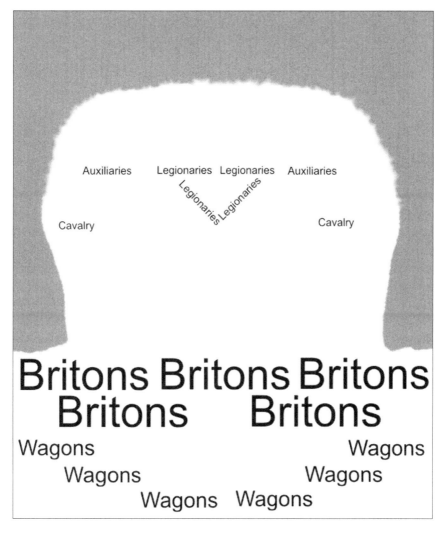

10 Boudica's final battle

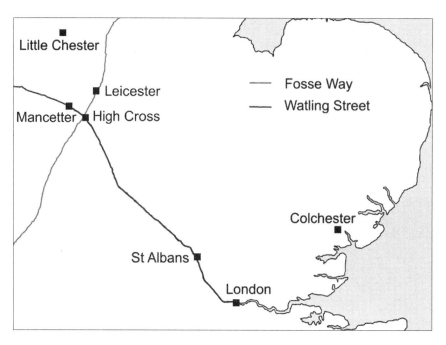

11 Possible locations of Boudica's final battle

army's momentum and harness the enthusiasm generated by their recent triumphs. If she had not pursued the governor, it could have been perceived that she was running from a fight, suggesting that she may not have been as powerful as her followers thought she was. She had promised them victory and she had to deliver. Boudica was not an experienced commander but she may have thought that it was prudent to engage Suetonius Paulinus before he had a chance to receive reinforcements. The early success of the rebel army had persuaded many to join their ranks and as the queen moved into position for battle, she may have hoped for, or have been promised, more tribal support further afield. Her forces were probably eager to confront the waiting Romans and so, laden down with worldly possessions, dependants and plunder, the Boudican hordes made their way north.

The site of the final battle is unknown, but Mancetter in North Warwickshire and High Cross in Leicestershire have both been suggested (Fig. 11). As the two armies faced each other, their commanders must have rallied their troops. The ancient sources give the opposing leaders suitably inspiring speeches with Tacitus' Boudica claiming that she is 'descended from mighty men' (Tacitus, *Annals*, 14.35). One wonders if Elizabeth I read Tacitus: 'I know I have the body of a weak and feeble woman, but I have the heart and stomach of a king, and a king of England too'. This famous quote from her Tilbury speech as she waited for the Spanish Armada invokes a similar theme and one she was fond of revisiting, as she also remarked: 'I may not be a lion, but I am a lion's cub, and I have a lion's heart'. If British tribes were used to having women war captains, then would it really have been necessary to invoke an impressive male lineage? Tacitus obviously thought so if Boudica was to stir her army's blood. Descendants were important to both Roman and Briton alike. Balsdon (1979) describes a distinguished Roman man's household having a picture gallery (*tablinum*) containing the family tree and death masks of all his ancestors, and Suetonius relates how the Emperor Caligula abhorred the idea of being the grandson of the great general Agrippa, because he had humble origins. Instead he preferred to think that his mother had been born out of wedlock, the product of an incestuous union between his grandmother Julia and her father, the Emperor Augustus (Suetonius, *Caligula*, 23).

Boudica is said to have practised a rite of divination before battle commenced by releasing a hare and reading the omens from the course it took. Dio concludes that it bolted in an auspicious direction and that the tribal armies cheered with delight in the knowledge that their cause was blessed (*Roman History*, 62.6.1-2). The fact that Boudica invoked the goddess Andraste, that hares were thought to have spiritual significance to the Britons (Collingridge, 2005, 237-8), and that she employed such a method of interpreting the will of her tribal deities has led to the suggestion that the queen was a priestess of her tribe and probably a Druidess as well (Ross, 1999). If she had been a member of the religious order, it may explain her ability to draw so many different followers to her and to be accepted as their leader (Ross & Robins, 1989). Female Druids were known in antiquity: Veleda, a prophetess who achieved prominence during Civilis' Batavian rebellion in AD 69 is thought to have been of the Druid caste and the women on the shores of Anglesey that so unnerved the approaching Roman soldiers could also have been part of the religious order.

Boudica's army would have been quite a sight to behold. Apart from their sheer numbers, her people would have been resplendent in a variety of outfits. The more traditional individuals may have been painted with symbolic designs to protect themselves in battle or could have been covered in woad and lime. The nobility would be likely to have elaborately decorated shields and helmets and those who had served abroad or with the Roman Army may even have had armour. There would be a large number of farmers and peasants there to protect their homes and possibly only armed with their tools for tilling the land. With the sounds of their war trumpets, the shouts of encouragement from their families, the rallying cries of the warriors and the thundering of the chariots, the outnumbered Romans must have been unnerved.

Willing to die, sword in hand and to be hailed as the hero in tribal songs passed down through generations, Boudica's forces had the best motivation of all. They may have looted and plundered, some may have joined just for the spoils of war and had no interest in fighting for freedom, but these people were fighting on their own soil, the earth they revered, watched by their loved ones and their ancestors. To die there would have been a noble death and to win would have given honour to themselves, their tribe and their gods. It was to be hoped that their passion and the size of their army could make up for what they lacked in coherence and discipline. This was not a force that regularly trained together and there was no permanent structure of command. Though strong on a one-to-one fighting basis and with the element of surprise, the Britons could not conduct complicated manoeuvres and faced with a force of disciplined, practised troops who could execute different commands at a pre-arranged trumpet signal; it is a testament to the native forces that they gave the Romans so much tough combat (Salway, 1981).

The Britons would have expended quite a bit of energy running up the slope towards the wooded defile. Suetonius Paulinus and his troops waited for the attack before throwing their javelins at close range. These weapons could not be removed from the British shields and so many would have discarded their only protection. The soldiers then advanced in wedge formation, using their shields to batter the rebels before stabbing them with their short swords, in a continuous forwards motion. In the bottleneck that developed, the rebels could not retreat and many were so tightly packed in that they could not effectively swing their swords. Their advancing numbers pressed them towards the Roman steamroller and their own wagons hemmed them in at the rear. Brought to the battleground to watch the fighting, the lines of carts filled with native families and trailing livestock meant that the hard-pressed warriors had no clear escape route and many were trampled and crushed in the chaos that ensued. Tacitus describes the outcome as slaughter on a massive scale – women and even the baggage animals were said to have been put to the sword. He reports that for the small number of 400 Roman dead, a huge 80,000 Britons were slain (Tacitus, *Annals*, 14.37). Great fighting force or not, as de la Bédoyère (2001, 69) points out, the Romans would have needed machine guns to clear those sorts of numbers. There is no doubt that an overwhelming number of Boudica's followers died on the battlefield, but Dio suggests that the victory may not have been so easily won and that many of the casualties were those non-combatants by the wagons. After lengthy fighting, the Romans were finally said to triumph, slaying many and taking others as prisoners, but 'not a few' are said to have fled the field and were 'preparing to fight again' (Dio, *Roman History*, 62.12.5-6), only finally admitting defeat after Boudica grew sick and died. Tacitus gives her the death of suicide by poison, recalling the demise of other 'barbarian queens', Cleopatra and Sophonisba. Did the Roman author imagine that Boudica would also wish to avoid the degradation of being paraded through the streets of the capital, as it seems strange that he would credit her with wanting to die honourably after losing her fight against Rome? The truth is we do not know what happened to the Icenian queen and her daughters. She may have been slaughtered in the battle, another bloody body littering the field, or she could have escaped with her family and the other refugees away from the Imperial retribution that would surely rain down. She may have become sick – used to a palace lifestyle, months in the field may not have suited her – or she could have received a wound that became infected. Whatever her fate, she has been remembered.

4

Revolt and Annexation
(AD 61–74)

The aftermath of the Boudican rebellion saw further casualties. On hearing of the Roman victory, Poenius Postumus, the temporary commander of Legion II *Augusta*, who had ignored his superior's request for assistance and lost his men a share in the glory, fell on his sword in disgrace. The tribal territories of the Iceni and Trinovantes felt the governor's full fury. Settlements were burned, buildings demolished and the people killed or taken as slaves. Boudica had denied Suetonius Paulinus his ultimate trophy – she must have been known to be dead or presumed so, otherwise she would have been hunted down with any other remaining rebels. If the queen had been slaughtered in battle, it would not have been an act for a soldier to be proud of and may even have been the result of disobeying a direct order – as such, it would not have been made public knowledge. A fate much worse than flogging would have awaited Boudica in Rome – she would not have received the merciful exile given to Caratacus. Death by her own hand, at a place of her choosing, surrounded by what was left of her people could have been her final act of control. Maybe her goddess of victory demanded her life as the price of her failure and as an offering, to ensure that her daughters escaped unharmed.

Waite (2007, 194) describes how the great enemy of Rome, Hannibal, chose suicide rather than capture in his old age, when after years of unending pursuit, the Romans found him hiding in exile. In escaping, Boudica would have had to put herself at the mercy of other tribal leaders and in the frenzy that followed the battle, the reward for her capture would have been great and the cost of sheltering her far too high – betrayal would be inevitable unless she removed herself from the Romans' reach. The highlands of Scotland were still unconquered, as was Ireland, but unless she had any family ties to recommend her, she would not have lasted long in hiding with no wealth for bribes. Anything not stolen by the Imperial agents could have been buried for safekeeping or would have been on the wagons that halted her retreat. It is possible that any remaining Druids could have aided her escape, but to say more would be to enter the realms of speculation.

Suetonius Paulinus may have secured a victory, but he had come close to disaster. Romans and loyal Britons had been massacred, three settlements had been ravaged and largely destroyed, and subject tribes who would have paid taxes to the Imperial treasury were now dead, or enslaved. Nero's advisors would not be singing the governor's praises. According to Dio (*Roman History*, 62.1.1), '... eighty thousand of the Romans and their allies perished, and the island was lost to Rome. Moreover, all this ruin was brought upon the Romans by a woman, a fact which itself caused them the greatest shame'. Suetonius Paulinus should never have left on campaign without providing for the possibility of trouble. Colchester should have been able to be defended by the colonists until reinforcements arrived, there should have been a better system of communication with the subordinate officers left in command and some sort of contingency plans should have been in place. Boudica had made an error in aiming at the Romans in a frontal assault, but different tactics could have ended the Imperial control of the province. Suetonius Paulinus was lucky and the emperor would have been made fully aware of this. The brutal excesses of Decianus Catus and his men would not have been an issue, as although they were the spark that ignited the inferno, his collectors were no doubt told to use whatever force was necessary and abuses against the natives were seen as an acceptable part of Roman occupation abroad.

In supposedly hunting down any remaining rebels, Suetonius Paulinus wreaked his revenge on the entire population. Already weakened by hunger as the harvests had been neglected in the conflict, the burning of the remaining farms and crops caused a famine that led to more deaths, especially those of the surviving sick, elderly and very young. The new procurator, Alpinus Classicianus, did not approve of the harshness of the governor's post-war actions – according to Tacitus, he threatened Roman interests by advising the remaining British rebels to wait until a new and more sympathetic governor was appointed before surrendering themselves and their arms (Tacitus, *Annals*, 14.38). The Roman author accuses him of settling private grievances by sending an unfavourable report of Suetonius Paulinus' conduct back to Rome, but as an admirer of the governor, Tacitus was likely to form this conclusion (Holland, 2000, 136). Alpinus Classicianus could well have had sympathy for the conquered people as he was a provincial himself, but humanitarian feelings aside, he would have been aware that the further suffering inflicted on the people would affect the tax revenues he had to send back to Rome even more. If Nero had just dismissed the Roman commander, he risked unpopularity with the army and possibly the Senate, so he sent one of his civil servants, a freedman named Polyclitus to assess the situation. After a brief interval, the loss of a few ships on the coast of Britain provided a pretext to recall Suetonius Paulinus. He was replaced in AD 61 by Petronius Turpilianus, a general who had just completed a term of office as Imperial Consul. The arrival of the new governor saw the end of the revolt and began the long process of recovery.

IMPACT OF THE REVOLT

Neutrality was not a guarantee of favour – those tribes that had not shown steadfast loyalty also felt the force of Roman retribution. If the fate of the rebels was not enough of a deterrent, the presence of reinforcements from Germany and tightened security measures were meant to show the surviving Britons in the province that they would never again be given the opportunity to resist Roman control. Cogidubnus and Cartimandua's kingdoms would have been spared the violent military response and they may even have been rewarded for their continued loyalty to Rome. In deciding to maintain such a position, both rulers took a considerable risk, as the rebellion threatened both of their territories. Had the rebels had turned south after the sacking of London or a little further north past the postulated battle site, then the pro-Roman monarchs could have faced a similar response to the 'collaborators' of St Albans.

It is unlikely that any native treaty with Rome would include sending troops to aid a struggling Roman commander and even more unlikely that Suetonius Paulinus would have asked the tribes for help. The Empire had been built on the ability to protect those people who showed their allegiance and to conquer those who refused. Although occasionally utilising the strength of other country's troops, Rome had to maintain a position of strength to keep attracting alliances and deterring enemies from attacking on multiple fronts (Braund, 1988, 92). Rather than providing active support, it may have been enough to know that if the struggle had reached their borders, Cartimandua and Cogidubnus would deploy their native forces in Rome's favour. Had one or both of the pro-Roman leaders decided to fight with Boudica, then the rebellion would probably have succeeded. With the

Brigantes as enemies, the Romans could have been surrounded, cut off from possible retreat or support from reinforcements, and the conflict could have lasted much longer and had a vastly different outcome.

Cartimandua had again chosen the path of co-operation with Rome when, as with Caratacus, her support could have changed the fate of the entire country. She was no 'fair weather friend' – reports of the scale of the Boudican revolt must have painted a very dim picture of the possibility of Roman success and yet the queen did not change sides in the conflict. It could be argued that in her own interests, Cartimandua could have joined the stronger force that looked most likely to triumph, but she had shown herself to be politically astute in the past and both she and her advisors would have looked at the bigger picture. If Boudica had failed even with Cartimandua's support, then the Brigantes would have shared in the brutality shown to rebelling tribes and the tribal queen would have lost her throne and her lands, her people their liberty or their lives. Had the union succeeded, the northern kingdom would have been no better off anyway – the Roman subsidies would stop and she would have no military support against her enemies. In allying herself with the anti-Roman army, it could be said that her people would have no reason to rebel and so she would not need Imperial reinforcements, but in the aftermath of the revolt, once the adrenaline had worn off, her people would face hardship. If Cartimandua shared her Roman wealth with the people, then they would have lost this income; if she did not share the benefits of friendship with Rome, then they would be further taxed to make up the shortfall – either way, it was the people and not just their queen who would be affected.

The tribal federation by its very nature was always going to be prone to internal fighting and rival factions, so the threat of conflict was always likely and tough times would only increase this possibility. Adding the uncertainty that Roman defeat would inevitably bring, the resulting tensions of 'victory' would not have seemed that appealing. Success also depended on the slim chance of Rome abandoning the province as Nero had wanted to do, deciding that it was much more trouble than it was worth. If Rome was to rethink the country's occupation, it is unlikely that such a step would be taken in defeat. Their reputation as a powerful Empire would be massively dented if, once conquered by the barbarians, Rome had been driven out of Britain altogether. Honour would demand a massive counter-attack and having spent many years as an ally of Rome (maybe even having spent some time there herself), Cartimandua would have known this. So with success would have come, at best, the chance to remain as queen, but a poorer, less powerful one at that, and at worst, the long wait for the terrible fury of Rome to descend. Her only chance to retain the power and position she and her people were used to was to risk continued friendship with Rome when many others refused to do so. Again, not a 'patriotic' stance, but she was not queen of Britain. She had never given the Romans an excuse to take her lands and as long as peace reigned in her kingdom, so did she.

Calm in Brigantia largely depended on Cartimandua's ex-consort, Venutius. After his unsuccessful attempt to invade the kingdom, he is not mentioned by the sources for another 12 years at least. If he was so determined to oppose Roman rule after his divorce and had the people on his side, then why did he not join with Boudica in her fight against the Empire? The Icenian revolt occurred some time between three and nine years after Venutius' attack on his former home. He had been defeated by Roman forces coming to the aid of his ex-wife, but he must have been aware that Suetonius Paulinus' troops were heavily outnumbered by the native army – he would be in no position to send help north. Venutius could have attacked Cartimandua's base without fear of an Imperial bodyguard and he could even have used his famed tactical skills to support Boudica and her followers, so why did he not act on this opportunity? As mentioned previously and explored in more detail shortly, there is an ongoing debate as to whether there were two Brigantian rebellions – one some time between AD 51 and AD 57 and the second in AD 69 – or whether Tacitus had made a mistake in duplicating his narrative. In Hanson and Campbell's view, Venutius' lack of response to Cartimandua being effectively unprotected by Roman arms suggests that there was only one rebellion and that it occurred in AD 69 (Hanson & Campbell, 1986, 79-80). This would mean that Venutius was still married to the Brigantian queen and happily enjoying their pro-Roman alliance in AD 60 at the time of the Boudican Revolt, explaining why he did not renew hostilities when the chance arose.

There are several other explanations for any lack of action. Hopeless romantics may suggest that even with the violence of their separation, Venutius was still hoping for a reconciliation, especially as he did not cause trouble for his ex-wife again until he was replaced in her affections by another man. It seems strange to rationalise events on such a large scale by looking at personal feelings, but power and position aside, this was a marriage between two fallible people and many wars in history have been fought over such emotional concerns. Cartimandua could have made an agreement with her former husband. He had been content to share the rewards of her pro-Roman stance for many years whilst they were married, so if she continued to share some of the benefits with him, he could have accepted 'alimony' and peace instead of the threat of Roman revenge and a life in hiding. Venutius may have been popular with certain factions, but in order to attempt a further attack, he would have needed to replenish his forces. The people may have been tired of conflict and longed for stability and security. Their queen seemed to have the approval of the gods as challenges to her regime continued to be deflected – she may even have held the religious title of priestess of her tribe as Boudica was thought to have done, although it is unlikely that Cartimandua was a Druidess if the order had supported Caratacus and possibly even encouraged the uprising in Brigantia in AD 47. Perhaps the massacre of the priesthood in Anglesey had ended their interference in her kingdom and Venutius had lost a powerful ally in persuading the Brigantes to his cause.

If he was skilled in military matters, the ex-consort could have been cautiously waiting to see the outcome of Boudica's campaign, as many other avenues of support were doing, before committing himself to any action. It is doubtful that Boudican messengers would have approached him in their mission to recruit supporters anyway – he was too far north to be of immediate assistance, he would have had to cross a large expanse of Brigantian territory unnoticed to join up with the rebels and he had not helped Caratacus when the fight was much nearer his own door. Any members of the Catuvellauni fighting with the anti-Roman army may have resented Venutius' neutrality at best or involvement in their prince's capture at worst. Moreover, Boudica was another woman in control – a reminder of the life he had been forced to leave. Any alliance with the Icenian rebels would involve being subordinate to her decisions and he may not have wanted to share the glory of the fight. If he had knowledge of Roman battle tactics, he may have foreseen the flaws in the native offensive and believed, as his former wife did, that their cause was doomed. The most likely explanation for his refusal to take advantage of the Roman absence, however, is that Cartimandua still held his family hostage. To retain her throne in uncertain times and allied to a force of men who resented her position, the queen would have been wise to trust no-one. Keeping her husband's relatives as security against his good behaviour, given his past actions, would have been a prudent decision. She may even have taken the added insurance of making new or strengthening existing bonds within the tribal alliance to safeguard her position against further internal assault. Venutius could have been ill, have left the country or have wanted to lick his wounds for a while – it could have been none of the above reasons or a combination of any one of them that led to him biding his time.

CALM IN BRITAIN, CONFLICT IN ROME

For almost a decade after the Boudican rebellion, Brigantia had peace. Her people had seen what had happened to those who resisted Rome and lost, and much as she may have been unpopular in some quarters, Cartimandua had protected them from this fate. Like the Iceni, they could have had their lands and assets stripped from them, their precious horses confiscated, their religious sites annihilated and their loved ones killed or taken as slaves. Old grievances may have remained, but they simmered gently rather than flaring up under white heat. The Romans seemed to have learnt their lesson and began to focus on consolidation rather than hasty expansion. Criticised by Tacitus for his 'inactivity', the governor Petronius Turpilianus led no military campaigns in his brief time in Britain. Needed in Rome, he was replaced in AD 63. His successor, Trebellius Maximus continued this policy of recovery and fortification, supervising the rebuilding of the devastated province and the fragile relationships with the native tribes. A new settlement was built at Colchester, 'the colony of the victorious' (Colonia Victricensis), complete with a thick defending wall which stood 4m high in parts, but the towns of London and St Albans did not begin real reconstruction until the AD 70s (Sealey, 2004, 52-6).

The events in Britain did not long distract the emperor, however, as his domestic life became increasingly eventful. The murder of his mother in AD 59 had begun his freedom from restraint, but in spite of constant pressure from his then mistress, Poppaea, he did not wish to risk unpopularity with the people by divorcing his wife (and Claudius' daughter), Octavia. This move was supported by his long-term advisor, Burrus – in discussing the possibility of a separation, he was said to have remarked 'Well then, give her back her dowry' (Dio, *Roman History*, 62.13.1), referring to the Imperial throne, for Octavia was Claudius' natural child and Nero merely his stepson and adopted heir. However, caution was then cast aside as his two mentors left his service in AD 62. Burrus died after developing a tumour in this throat, although the sources suggest that Nero had him poisoned (Suetonius, *Nero*, 35; Dio, *Roman History*, 62.13.3) – Tacitus mentions the common belief that the emperor ordered his murder, but acknowledges that it could also have been natural causes (Tacitus, *Annals*, 14.51). Seneca resigned shortly afterwards and the last guiding hand to advise moderation was gone. The emperor's honest and politically shrewd advisors were effectively replaced by Tigellinus, an unscrupulous and violent man who encouraged Nero in his excesses. It was quite a year for the young emperor. Free to make his own decisions without the disapproval of his learned counsellors, Nero exiled and then murdered his popular first wife, Octavia, so that he could marry the pregnant Poppaea and produce a legitimate heir. His daughter Claudia Augusta was born the next year, but she died within four months.

Many were to follow her, as the Great Fire killed untold masses in Rome in AD 64. Palaces, public buildings, homes, temples, shrines and much of the Imperial collection of art and history were destroyed. Nero was blamed for the occurrence with the sources describing a varied degree of involvement and guilt. Tacitus tells us that although the emperor was not even in the city when the fire broke out and that he helped in the relief effort and showed charity to the destitute, many people believed that Nero had ordered the fire to be started so that he could found a new city. Such views were encouraged by the rumours that gangs of armed men had sabotaged any attempts to battle the flames and that a new outbreak of fire, starting when the crisis was subsiding, began on the estate of Tigellinus, Nero's henchman (Tacitus, *Annals,* 15.38-40). Suetonius has Nero setting fire to the city himself, whilst Dio allows that he sent his minions out secretly to begin the devastation (Suetonius, *Nero,* 38; Dio, *Roman History,* 62.16.2). However, all three sources mention the famous image of Nero singing as he watched Rome burn. Holland is keen to debunk this myth and suggest that the emperor could have been falsely accused. He details Nero's extensive efforts in directing the rescue forces and explains that the emperor's new palace was eventually located some distance from the site he is supposed to have destroyed to make way for a replacement. In addition, he makes the point that in rushing from Actium in the dead of night, Nero is unlikely to have thought it handy to grab a musical instrument and relevant costume on the off-chance he got to have a good jamming session (Holland, 2000, 171-5). It could be that the emperor was not involved – the men stopping the fire-fighters could have been keen on looting undisturbed, rather than following orders to advance the destruction (Tacitus, *Annals,* 15.38). It would have been a little stupid of Tigellinus to start a fire in his own grounds if Nero had wanted to deny any involvement in the disaster – it is more likely that the Imperial bully was detested by the people and some disgruntled Roman saw an opportunity to take revenge for his cruel treatment. Whatever the cause of the fire, there were further casualties as Nero chose the 'depraved' Christian sect as scapegoats for the crime – in a sea of crucifixions, burnings and people ripped apart by dogs, the emperor misjudged the effect of these barbaric displays and even lost his popularity with the common people (Tacitus, *Annals,* 15.44). The inhabitants of Rome will no doubt have believed that their gods were displeased with them, but for the conquered people of

Britain, the destruction of the Imperial capital would have seemed like divine retribution.

Nero's reputation never really recovered from the fire and its aftermath, but instead of strengthening his support among the troops that he had never led into battle, the emperor began to indulge his artistic interests at the expense of damage limitation. He refused to appreciate how much his people had been alienated by his over-spending and neglect, and even after a conspiracy to eliminate him was foiled in AD 65, unleashing a terrible onslaught of torture, executions and forced suicides, Nero did nothing to win back popularity. The emperor asked one of his Praetorian Guard, Subrius Flavius, why he had joined the conspirators against him and acted contra to his oath of loyalty as an Imperial soldier and was told: 'Because I detested you! I was as loyal as any of your soldiers as long as you deserved affection. I began detesting you when you murdered your mother and wife and became charioteer, actor and incendiary!' (Tacitus, *Annals*, 15.67). Even this blunt declaration did nothing to inspire Nero to change his ways in the realisation that he was in danger. It was just a matter of time before rebellion occurred.

The trouble began in AD 68 in a province of Gaul (Gallia Lugdunensis). Led by the governor, Vindex, who was himself of Gallic origin, a move to depose Nero was supported by Galba, the governor of Northern Spain (Fig. 12). Despite rumoured negotiations with Rufus, the governor of Upper Germany, Vindex was defeated by the Rhine soldiers and later committed suicide after many of his men were killed. Rufus's troops repeatedly offered him the throne, but he famously refused, leaving the way open for Galba to claim the purple. Nero's support melted away as his replacement marched to Rome. The governor had already been proclaimed emperor by his troops (Dio, *Roman History*, 63.23), but he was then recognised by the Senate as the new ruler of the Empire. The fugitive Nero committed suicide with the help of his secretary, the freedman Epaphroditus, and thus ended the Julio-Claudian dynasty. It was followed by the chaos of a civil war, with AD 69 being dubbed 'the Year of the Four Emperors'.

THE 'SECOND' BRIGANTIAN REBELLION

Galba knew that the Rhine legions had loyally supported Nero in opposing Vindex and he saw this as an attempt to halt his accession. The emperor replaced Rufus and appointed Vitellius as governor of Lower Germany, after his predecessor was assassinated by his own men.

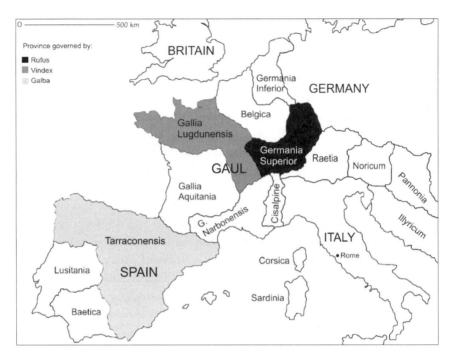

12 Roman Europe – Year of The Four Emperors

Galba had alienated many in his treatment of the people, but especially the army, as he reneged on his promise to reward the troops who had allowed him to arrive safely in Rome and he did nothing to soothe the tensions in Germania. This resulted in Vitellius being hailed as sovereign by the soldiers in his new command, proving, as Galba himself had done, that it was possible 'for an emperor to be chosen outside Rome' (Tacitus, *Histories*, 1.4). This news prompted the elderly emperor to name his successor, rejecting the ambitious and influential Otho, the governor of Lusitania who had joined Galba in his march to Rome in AD 68 (he was also the man Poppaea had divorced once she became Nero's mistress). Otho persuaded the disgruntled Praetorian Guard to his side and when Galba took to the streets in an attempt to rally support, he was murdered in the Forum. The year had got off to a bloody start. Otho was proclaimed emperor by the Senate but his rival, Vitellius had begun to advance his army towards Rome.

The army was divided in their loyalty to the two leaders. In Britain, Legions II *Augusta*, IX *Hispana* and XX *Valeria* sent troops to support Vitellius. Legion XIV *Gemina* had been ordered to go east by Nero shortly before his death, but they, like the Praetorian Guard, favoured Otho (Frere, 1987). The lack of military expansion and opportunities to plunder in the province had left the army restless and the feud between the governor and the commander of Legion XX, Roscius Coelius led to a mutiny (Tacitus, *Histories*, 1.60). Trebellius Maximus fled to Vitellius, who had become emperor after Otho killed himself in defeat following a battle at Bedriacum in Northern Italy. The troubled governor was not restored to his post, as the emperor sent Vettius Bolanus as a replacement. Vitellius later ordered the defiant Legion XIV *Gemina* back to Britain in an attempt to smooth tensions in the army, but after only a few months of wearing the Imperial purple, he learnt that many other discontented legions had sworn allegiance to Vespasian, the governor of Judaea, and were hailing him as the new emperor. Letters were sent from the rebels to the Fourteenth Legion in Britain as they had supported Otho against Vitellius, but support was divided in the rest of the province's troops. Tacitus describes the majority favouring the new candidate, as he had distinguished himself in Britain as commander of Legion II *Augusta* under Claudius, but the high ranks in the other legions who owed their career success to Vitellius were uneasy about the thought of another change in leadership (Tacitus, *Histories*, 3.44).

In this environment of uncertainty at home and civil war abroad, with detachments of soldiers leaving the island, trouble broke out again in Brigantia. Having missed the opportunity to take advantage of the distraction provided by the Boudican rebellion, Venutius was not going to ignore a second chance. In examining this situation, it is necessary to rely on Tacitus' earlier work. In a process as confusing as adding the three extra prequel films to the *Star Wars* trilogy, Tacitus wrote about the events of AD 69 (*Histories*) before he went back and described what happened in Brigantia in the AD 50s (*Annals*). Perhaps George Lucas is a fan of the Roman author as there are similarities in their stories – the Rebel Alliance against the Empire, the royal female in command and the fetching uniforms worn by the Imperial forces. The intervening years between the two revolts seem not to have mellowed the queen's disgruntled ex-husband. Tacitus talks of Venutius' loyalty to Rome in the *Annals*, but he is later said to possess 'a violent character and a hatred of all things Roman' (Tacitus, *Histories*, 3.45). However, the Roman author does state that the fidelity was linked to his time as royal consort. It could be argued that he always had a bit of an aggressive nature, since he had invaded Brigantia on one occasion already. Defeat by the Roman forces may have engendered his hatred and he could also have blamed Cartimandua's alliance with Rome for the problems between them. Venutius may have always disapproved of his spouse's co-operation with the Empire, but like Boudica, he did nothing to challenge it during their marriage.

The famous warlord Caratacus was delivered into Roman hands without protest from the Brigantian 'king', but this could be said to have been in deference to his wife's wishes. Boudica rebelled on an enormous scale and Venutius was content to remain in exile up north. Years passed in peace and tranquillity, but the ex-consort did take up arms on two occasions – once when his wife divorced him and once when she decided to remarry. He was not exactly the poster-child for freedom fighting. Tacitus talks about Venutius' abhorrence of Rome before he mentions his constancy – it could be that after writing the *Histories*, the Roman author decided that the story would read better if the rejected husband discarded his long-time allegiance to the Empire because of his wife. Cartimandua could be blamed for the whole incident and Tacitus was free to indulge in another spot of criticism of a woman ruling alone. Far from having legitimate reasons for ending her long-term marriage, Cartimandua is said to succumb to self-gratification as a result of her new affluent lifestyle (Tacitus, *Histories*, 3.45).

Tacitus' comments would seem to be inspired by women much closer to his own back yard, as the decadence of the Roman nobility and certainly some of its empresses was legendary. The ancient Britons were supposedly hedonistic anyway – they were said to have loved to feast, fight, hunt, ride and display their good fortune in bright clothes, jewellery and accessories. Subsidies from Rome would not really have changed all that – it just enabled the high-status goods to be bought or commissioned from further afield. Tacitus was writing at the beginning of the rule of the 'Five Good Emperors' (a concept introduced by Machiavelli and popularised by Edward Gibbon). With benevolent rulers and their virtuous wives (if they were married at all) in power in Rome, it is no wonder that Tacitus chose to focus on the sensationalised love life of a barbarian queen many years earlier, for as gossip magazines and inferior newspapers today have discovered: sex sells. Boudica could not be cast in the role of temptress – she had the part of the 'ill-treated mother/widow' in Tacitus' narrative, so whilst she was defending her home and her battered honour in an unladylike fashion, Cartimandua was seen to explore her own selfish desires.

The catalyst for the trouble that was to erupt was a man named Vellocatus, who became the Brigantian queen's second husband. Modern sources have often described the 'affair' between Cartimandua and her new love, accusing her of adultery. This stems from varying translations of the passage in Tacitus' *Annals* (12.40) which describes the initial estrangement of Venutius and his wife several years before. Grant (1996) talks of a 'divorce' occurring, whereas others categorise the fight as a 'quarrel', but the description of the disagreement in these sources is prefaced by the statement that Venutius was only loyal to Rome when he was married to the tribal queen. As civil war is then said to break out, it can be assumed that they are no longer together. In either case, it would seem that the relationship is over at least 12 years before she makes Vellocatus her consort, which she is perfectly at liberty to do without committing any sort of infidelity. A lawful second marriage is not as interesting a topic as a scandalous extra-marital fling, however, and so again Cartimandua is portrayed in a negative light, whether it is deserved or not.

Tacitus tells us that Vellocatus was formerly Venutius' armour-bearer and that in elevating him to the position of royal companion, Cartimandua made a reckless decision: 'this scandal immediately shook the royal house to its foundations' (Tacitus, *Histories*, 3.45). It has been suggested that it is the new consort's previous position that caused outrage in the kingdom. Webster assumes that Vellocatus was of 'servile status' (1993a, 89-90), but as Braund points out, if Tacitus had believed him to be a servant or slave, he would have had a field day in describing the degradation attached to a royal liaison with such a lowly person (Braund, 1984b, 3, n.8). Juvenal describes a senator's wife running off with a gladiator (Juvenal, *Satire 6*, 82-113) and it was this apparent taste for common men which gripped the moralists and writers in their descriptions of faithless aristocratic wives (D'Ambra, 2007, 49). *Satire 6* has often been used as an example of Juvenal's misogyny, but as Balsdon explains 'in the language of hate and scorn, women cannot expect better treatment than is accorded to the rest of society which, in the satirist's clever distortion, both shared and encouraged their degradation' (Balsdon, 1977, 16). Braund agrees with this assessment, believing that all, but especially 'out-groups', are fair game for the satirist's invective – their work is often based on extreme characters that are exaggerated to explore an issue, in Juvenal's case in *Satire 6*, that of whether or not a man should marry (Braund, 1992, 85-6). It is only the work of the *male* writers, poets and satirists that has survived though – we do not have a Roman woman's point of view.

It is much more likely that Vellocatus was of noble birth. In antiquity, the position of armour-bearer was a prestigious one and it is still listed as one of the Great Offices of the Royal Household in Scotland. Although a largely ceremonial role in modern times, it was historically very influential. An armiger (Tacitus used the word '*armigerum*') today is a person entitled to use a coat of arms, but originally this armour-bearer or squire would be 'honoured, of high birth and achievement' (Turnbull & Fitts, 1988, 381). It has been suggested that the Romans would still consider a formal relationship between a hereditary queen and her ex-husband's subordinate as shameful (Collingridge, 2005, 146), but short of marrying another tribal king, anyone by those standards would be considered so. This seems unlikely, however, as many of the Roman emperors were not sons of royalty and it would seem very hypocritical for a Roman audience to judge the potential suitors of a foreign 'barbarian queen' with higher standards than for their own Imperial families. In any case, the scandal was said to be among her own people and not from a Roman point of view. We do not know what ancient Brigantians would have considered proper in choosing a husband for their queen – if it was a warrior culture, a great fighter who was of lowly origins may have been suitable if bravery was seen as a more valuable characteristic than noble blood. However, Vellocatus likely had both as Venutius' 'most trusted client-chief' (Richmond, 1954, 52). Thus, if public outrage was not caused by Vellocatus' background or his former position, then why was the royal household so devastated by Cartimandua's new marriage? Turnbull and Fitts believe the target for the disapproval to be the actual divorce itself, as the separation of two such powerful individuals could have affected the entire nobility and the royal house's claims to sovereignty in the tribal federation (Turnbull & Fitts, 1988, 381). This may well be true, but no more so than civil war between the rival factions would have done. For Brigantian society to be rocked in such an immediate way, it would take a drastic move – like marrying a Roman.

As a monarch friendly to Rome, Cartimandua is likely to have been awarded Roman citizenship, or she may have inherited it if her predecessor was a direct family member who had ruled in sympathy with the Empire. If she or her family had spent some time in Rome, connections could have been formed. Fostering was common in the ancient world – a position in a foreign royal household may have been a good experience for a young Roman noble, especially a second or third son, particularly if there had been some prior social link such as a marriage between the two families. If a native Roman occupied a prime position in her husband's entourage, what better way for Cartimandua to display her loyalty to Rome on a personal level? It may also have had Imperial encouragement as it could be seen as a guarantee of honest communication if one of their own was part of the powerful household. If Venutius had developed an abhorrence of anything Roman, it would make sense for Vellocatus to remain in the royal household and not follow him into exile. Although if this was not the case, Venutius could have desired his reliable squire to remain with the queen as a way of gaining intelligence – for him to then be replaced by his former courtier as consort would have been painful. Richmond believes that Cartimandua's choice of a new husband could have been as much political as personal. He considers that the timing of the nuptials (with Venutius posing a real threat in wanting revenge) and the queen's perceptive assessment of the growing conflict, both in Rome and at home, could have meant that in gaining a husband she may well have loved, she would also be depriving her ex-partner of a trusted and capable ally. Such marriages were common in Roman aristocratic circles and yet, as Richmond shrewdly observes, Tacitus treats the fact that Cartimandua chooses such a path as a moral issue (Richmond, 1954, 52).

It could be argued that if Vellocatus had been Roman then Tacitus would have mentioned it. He may not have known about it as he was probably working from older source material, but if he did, he may have judged it unwise to include such a detail in the passage. Romans were fascinated by the 'otherness' of barbarian cultures – it may not have had the same dramatic impact to find that one of their own was involved in this foreign gossip. Alternatively, Vellocatus' name may have led Tacitus' audience to assume that he was Roman anyway. In Latin, '*vello*' means plucked or smooth and '*catus*' means sharp or cunning, but if de la Bédoyère (2003, 79) is correct in stating that '*bello*' would be seen as '*vello*' by a Latin reader ('*bello*' meaning to wage war or fight), then Vellocatus could be a 'cunning fighter' or a 'clean-shaven, sharp man'. Either of those meanings could have applied to a Roman armour-bearer.

Marriage to a Roman could have been the final straw for those factions in the Brigantian kingdom who had fought against an alliance with the Empire. Much as Cartimandua may have been a friend to Rome, she was still a tribal queen. Maybe these proud native elements had hoped for a return to a more traditional kingdom if civil war in Rome had meant a withdrawal of her forces from occupied territories. This marriage meant that the queen was never going to see things their way and according to Tacitus, her people were moved to an immediate show of displeasure. Intermarriage in any situation where one country has been conquered by another is always unpopular with purists on both sides, often attracting violent reprisals and accusations of collaboration as the couple are made outcasts in their respective communities. Nuptials between people of different faiths, races and nationalities still attract hostility in our supposedly liberal world today, as for some, little has changed in 2000 years in terms of attitude to change and tolerance. Cartimandua may have felt more comfortable with a Roman husband, given her position, her upbringing or even her aspirations and as her people had never been conquered by Rome, she did not have the wounds of conflict to heal; nevertheless, her choice of partner was universally frowned upon. Marriages undoubtedly occurred between Romans and native women, but not at this level of society. Supporters of Venutius would have seen the marriage as a betrayal of loyalty to him, if not from his ex-wife, then from his former squire. Those individuals who desired power for themselves may have resented another step towards permanent protection for their queen, as there is no suggestion that Rome disapproved of Cartimandua's choice of husband. This could have been another reason for Venutius to feel aggrieved – his squire was deemed more suitable as a royal consort than he was, despite being the leader of his own people and a respected military man.

Having remained on the Brigantian throne for at least 20 years at this point, Cartimandua had shown that she knew how to fortify her position, but she has been accused of showing a lapse in judgement in her decision to marry Vellocatus. It is unlikely that she believed such a move would be popular with her people – they had spent years showing their disapproval of her policy decisions. She may have known how popular her ex-husband was with her followers, which is why she chose to let him go into exile rather than being hunted by Roman forces. However, she had also made choices that were not meant to be universally liked. She had done what she thought was best for herself and her kingdom and, selfish or not, she still had her lands and her people had not had the humiliation of conquest. After years of peace, the spectre of conflict again loomed large and she had to protect herself in the most efficient way she could. Relying on the goodwill of a large group of rival parties that had shown themselves loyal to her enemies in the past would have been naïve at best. She had been forced to pick a side when Caratacus entered her lands and when Boudica rose up against Imperial rule, and on the two occasions when her own people had rebelled, Rome had honoured their alliance with her, so it was really a 'no-brainer'.

Much as Caratacus, Boudica, Venutius and the other British rebels did not see a favourable future for themselves in a Roman world, Cartimandua knew she did not have a real future outside of it. Even as a 'barbarian queen' co-operating with a male-dominated Empire, she held more power than many independent kings did. Her reign had shown the need to take risks to maintain her throne and they had ultimately paid off – strategically, a marriage to a candidate unacceptable to her people but favourable to Rome was just another gamble. She may even have been ruled by sentiment if this time her marriage was based on emotion rather than just dynastic considerations – as anyone in love knows, the consequences go right out of the window. It would have been a bonus if Vellocatus was desirable on a personal level, but it is unlikely that Cartimandua would make such a choice purely on passion – she had ruled without a consort for more than a decade and could have had an affair with him that her household would surely have known about. It is more probable that Tacitus could not fault Cartimandua for ruling like a queen so he suggested that she ruled like a woman, with her heart and not her head. This would be yet another example to his audience of why female rulers were a bad idea. Elizabeth I was in the same position for many years, having to put the needs of the State ahead of her own feelings – however, she famously never married.

The fact that there was an immediate reaction to this royal 'scandal' suggests that preparations had been made beforehand. Tacitus says that Venutius could 'rely on the support of the Brigantian people' (Tacitus, *Histories*, 3.45), but how would the rebel know this if he had not been planning to oppose his ex-wife again? Admittedly, Tacitus does not give an exact time frame, but things do appear to have progressed in rapid succession. It is likely that having gathered intelligence about the withdrawal of some Roman troops abroad and hearing of the mixed feelings within the remaining legions, Venutius had secretly entered into negotiations with the various factions in the Brigantian alliance. The queen may have discovered what was happening and the knowledge that her people planned to rebel again prompted her to take action for her own protection. Vellocatus may have had men of his own that he, and more importantly she, could rely on to support their position.

Circumstances must have changed for Venutius to feel safe in taking another rebellious stance – it is unlikely that his ex-wife had released his relatives at this time of uncertainty in Rome, as she would want to keep the hostages as leverage to guard against further attack. However, it is possible that they may have died, leaving Venutius free from fear of reprisals on them. Tacitus shows a distinct bias in summarising the events that followed. Venutius, having been 'discarded' is said to have had the loyalty of the Brigantes, whereas his former squire had only 'the infatuation of the queen and her ruthless cruelty' (Tacitus, *Histories*, 3.45). A proven rebel against Rome had again secretly planned to invade his former home, inciting the people to rise against their hereditary queen. Cartimandua had given Venutius the position and the influence that allowed him to curry their favour and yet she is painted as the villain of the piece. She had shown unwavering loyalty to Rome in the face of several opportunities to change her political stance. Caratacus was handed over to the Roman authorities after he attempted to incite rebellion and challenge Cartimandua's throne and when her long-term husband attempted to overthrow her in invading her kingdom, he was defeated and forced to withdraw. As a queen such behaviour is seen as 'ruthless', but if a king had taken such prudent steps to protect his birthright, he would be described as 'shrewd' and 'a force to be reckoned with'. He would be respected and his actions seen as totally justifiable. Where is the evidence of the queen's supposedly vindictive temperament? Why does Tacitus not elaborate further as he is not usually one for shying away from gossip and rumour? It is possible that Cartimandua is being portrayed here as a Poppaea or a Messalina, as it provides a much better contrast to the image of the wronged husband given to Venutius.

Caratacus had defied Rome for years and yet he was given a stirring speech. Cartimandua's support helped Rome to gain the glory of triumph in Britain and yet she is given disapproval. As a queen ruling for years alone and by hereditary entitlement, she was never going to be praised by the sources, regardless of her actions. Cartimandua may well have been calculating, she may have disregarded the wishes of her people and she could have taken steps that were considered harsh – like every other person involved in the events of the time, she was a flawed individual, making mistakes and enemies as anyone in such a position of power inevitably will. However, when censure is confined to the one person who has not shown herself to be particularly faithless or treacherous, the bias of the source must be acknowledged. The queen could have been a thoroughly unpleasant individual, but equally her people may have liked her and just detested her policies. Regardless of her personal appeal, her main crime according to Tacitus seems to have been her birthright and her gender.

The queen found herself in a position of assault from all sides. Venutius again attacked the kingdom with the help of external forces, but on this occasion it was set to coincide with an internal Brigantian revolt. He was taking no chances this time. In a position of serious peril, Cartimandua appealed to her Roman allies for help. Here, timing affected the outcome of events as it had done with many of the major turning points in Roman Britain so far. Prasutagus died at a point when Nero really needed a new source of wealth to fund his lavish expenditure, and the Icenian king was rumoured to be extremely rich. Had his death occurred at another time, the incident that lit the fuse of the Boudican rebellion may never have happened as the procurator may not have had the same pressure to provide spoils from Britain and might not have used such brutal measures to achieve his ends. Cunobelin died around the time that Claudius needed a military victory and Verica's flight to Rome gave the emperor an excuse to formalise the annexation of Britain.

Vettius Bolanus was cautious in his decision of which candidate for the purple to support – the existing emperor who had appointed him as governor of Britain or the popular Vespasian who looked likely to succeed to the throne. Although Vitellius had requested reinforcements from the provinces of Britain, Germany and Spain, all three governors were effectively dragging their feet rather than wanting to support a losing cause (Tacitus, *Histories*, 2.97). Birley states that whilst the fight for supremacy in the Empire persisted, the governor had no interest in controlling his own insubordinate troops or in dealing effectively with the enemy (Birley, 1976, 11). Tacitus definitely seemed to prefer men of action, describing Vettius Bolanus as having 'a hand too gentle for a warlike province' (Tacitus, *Agricola*, 8). He decides that the governor's decision not to impose discipline in Britain showed 'the same paralysis in the face of the foe', but in an attempt at mitigation says that he had 'won affection where he lacked authority' (Tacitus, *Agricola*, 16). Cartimandua may well have agreed with this assessment, although she probably was not feeling too affectionate towards him when he sent her auxiliary infantry and cavalry (*cohorts alaeque*), instead of a crack company of legionary troops.

There could have been several reasons for such a decision. De la Bédoyère postulates that these units may have been stationed nearest to the trouble, but he also mentions that the governor would not have wanted to gamble on sending a legion in such an uncertain situation (de la Bédoyère, 2003, 80). Vettius Bolanus may not have had any more men to send, depending on what part of the Year of the Four Emperors (AD 69) that the Brigantian conflict occurred. The struggle between Vitellius and his rival Vespasian may have taken precedence over an internal British conflict in terms of the deployment of reinforcements, especially as fresh trouble had broken out in Germany and Pontus (modern-day Turkey). The stability of the Brigantian kingdom had been of paramount importance to the Imperial administration, but now they were busy fighting fires of their own. Nevertheless, an important Roman ally could not be left unaided so Vettius Bolanus may have sent what troops he could risk in the hope that they would be enough to crush the rebels. Alternatively, with a power shift looking likely, it is possible that the governor had decided to tread water in Britain until he received orders from the undoubted victor in the battle for the Imperial throne. He may not have had the authority to act without orders and as his legions could have been a deciding factor in any future conflict, he would not have been popular if he had committed at least one of them elsewhere fighting ferocious natives. Whether unable or disinclined to act in a major way, he made the reasonably safe decision to put a metaphorical 'toe' in the 'waters' of Brigantian conflict. Thus, timing again dictated policy.

There is little doubt that the governor's choice of a rescue party lost Cartimandua her throne. Had a legionary force been sent, there could have been a very different result. We are not told how many rebels Venutius had managed to persuade or bribe to his cause and it may just have been that after years of peacetime, he was now prepared to mount an all-out attack, making complete use of his military skills. Like Boudica, he knew that he would not get another chance where the prevailing conditions were so much in his favour – the Romans had not turned their backs as they did with the Iceni, but they did have their hands effectively tied, preventing a full-scale campaign. He had to succeed, as a second unsuccessful revolt would not be treated mercifully. The Brigantes must have thought the gods were finally listening to them when they realised that Vettius Bolanus' legions were not being sent against them. Not to denigrate the rescue mission undertaken by the troops that were deployed, but the tribes had seen what a small force of disciplined legionaries could do against overwhelming odds. However, it was no easy victory. The auxiliaries encountered some 'desperate fighting' before they managed to extricate Cartimandua from the danger that her ex-husband's assault posed to her person (Tacitus, *Histories*, 3.45). It is likely that she would have been killed or held hostage as Venutius' family had been, so the decision must have been made at some point, when the chance of a total victory had disappeared, to prevent her from being trapped, get her out of the conflict and worry about the consequences to her position later. These could have been some of the same men who had rebelled against Trebellius Maximus and any continuance of their lack of discipline then could explain their limited success here (Wolfson, 2002, Part 5, n.325). If Cartimandua had been on the throne when Claudius annexed the province, her rule had lasted for at least 26 years – it was the end of an era in British history. The first hereditary queen that we know about had been overthrown.

THEORIES OF REBELLION

Narratives of the Brigantian uprisings are thought by some to be two similar descriptions of the same event. Written first, the *Histories* describes the Brigantian conflict of AD 69 (Tacitus, *Histories*, 3.45) – this is assumed to be the correct recollection of what occurred. In his later work, the *Annals*, which tackles an earlier period in time (AD 14 to AD 68), Tacitus is thought to have mistakenly placed a duplicate account of the revolt (Tacitus, *Annals*,

12.40). If this is the case, then the argument is that the troubles of the AD 50s in the Brigantian royal household did not exist – Cartimandua and Venutius stayed married until AD 69, when she spurned him for Vellocatus. It is assumed that of the two, the *Histories* is most likely to be the accurate account, as the explosive and uncertain political climate in AD 69 seems more suggestive of an opportune time for Venutius to rebel (Mitchell, 1978, 218). Support for the 'duplicate' theory is said to come from the fact that Tacitus had a reputation for carelessness in mentioning detail. He had already made an error in referring to Brigantian affairs, when he confused the Brigantes with the Iceni in Calgacus's speech in the *Agricola* (Tacitus, *Agricola*, 31), a book that was written before either the *Histories* or the *Annals*. Webster takes a slightly different approach to the idea of there being two narratives, but only one rebellion. He believes that although both descriptions relate to the same event, the *Histories* gives slightly more detail than the *Annals*, so he combines the two versions to form one rather confusing account of Cartimandua's break with Venutius (Webster, 1993a, 89-90) – the 'amalgamation' theory.

Hanson and Campbell agree with the idea that Tacitus may have made a mistake and suggest that the weaknesses of the 'reconciliation' theory increase the likelihood of there being only one rebellion. They point out that as the *Histories* talks about Cartimandua marrying the squire of her *husband*, Venutius, in AD 69, it implies that some sort of reunion occurred. If the two passages had related to separate events, it would mean that after their divorce in the AD 50s, the royal couple resolved their differences and remarried, before divorcing for the second time 12 or more years later (Hanson & Campbell, 1986, 78). Given the violence of their initial separation, this would indeed seem to be implausible. However, if a reconciliation did not happen between Cartimandua and Venutius after their initial divorce, the two passages may still be able to stand up as separate accounts of different rebellions (Fig. 13).

In examining this concept, it is necessary to address the points made in opposition to the possibility of two major instances of conflict in Brigantia. Firstly, Tacitus is said to show little concern for the specific names of people and places outside of Rome and is thought to prefer imagination to the strict boundaries of fact (Wellesley, 1954, 13). This may indeed be true, but it is important to bear in mind that a large portion of his work does not survive, so we do not have a comprehensive collection to examine. In addition, the fact that the works we do have are not original manuscripts could mean that some errors were committed by those individuals copying his books. Tacitus' readers would not have wanted extensive accounts of the

	ANNALS AD 51-57	*HISTORIES* AD 69	NUMBER OF REBELLIONS
Duplicate Theory	Incorrect placing	Correct placing	One
Amalgamation Theory	Incorrect placing but more detail	Correct placing	One
Reconciliation Theory	Correct placing	Correct placing but assumes remarriage and another divorce	Two
Flash-back Theory	Correct placing	Correct placing	Two

13 Theories about the Brigantian rebellions ▨ Incorrect ▨ Correct

tribes, sub-tribes and geography of Britain. As Hanson points out, 'upper class Romans, mostly knew little about outlying provinces and would undoubtedly have been bored by the use of too many strange sounding names' (Hanson, 1987, 21). It is also possible that if Tacitus was responsible for the error confusing the Brigantes with the Iceni in his *Agricola*, it is because he was not then in possession of all the information later at his disposal, as this description of Boudica's revolt differs from the account in the *Annals* (Burn, 1969, 40). One mistake involving the Brigantes does not mean that all references to them are suspect.

There are undoubted likenesses in the two passages describing the turbulent Brigantian royal household, but this does not necessarily mean that they must be recounting the same occurrence. It is entirely possible that the similarities in both pieces are the result of a 'flash-back' from the *Histories* to the earlier events of the AD 50s in the *Annals* (Braund, 1984b, 3). Tacitus sets the scene for the drama unfolding in AD 69 by describing the key players, Venutius and Cartimandua, telling his audience who they are and what their background is together. He then goes back to the events of AD 51 when Caratacus was captured, explaining how the queen was rewarded and how this affected her. The recall ends with the phrase 'spurning her husband Venutius' and Braund's 'flash-back' theory focuses on these words as the bridge between the two time periods. He points out that a reconciliation need not be supposed, as in tiring of her former spouse, she replaces him with his 'erstwhile armour-bearer', a phrase which emphasises Vellocatus' former position (Braund, 1984b, 3-4). In translating this passage in the *Histories*, Wellesley would seem to agree with the reading of Cartimandua's first marriage in the past tense, as he interprets the bridging phrase as 'She tired of Venutius, who was her consort'. Thus, the queen capturing Caratacus and the royal marriage breaking up are the two events that both Tacitus' passages have in common – the original recounting in the *Annals* and the flash-back to these incidents in the *Histories*. The Roman author may have already been planning the *Annals* when he wrote the *Histories* and so chose to go back to the earlier happenings to explain the animosity of the present and to pre-empt his narrative in the later book.

Apart from the common elements already mentioned, the similarities in the two passages could also be seen as an example of Tacitus' inclination towards self-imitation (Woodman, 1979, 143-55). However, although the author had been known to pad out certain sketchy events with details from more adequately documented incidents in other parts of his work, it was not a regular habit and can only be shown on a few occasions (Hanson, 1987, 17). Having acknowledged the flaws in his writing and any biases therein, we can compensate for such factors and feel free to appreciate his work as it is. Tacitus is often our only source in many cases and his books are a very useful example of ancient historical narratives, which follow the accepted practices of the day in giving opinion and rumour alongside the facts, and using invention to alter recorded events in order to present a more polished finish. In comparing the description in the *Histories* to those in its prequel, many more differences can be noted than points of similarity (Fig. 14). Venutius' approach to the Romans changes between the two events. As a result of the hostilities in the AD 50s, Cartimandua takes members of her former husband's family hostage; in the revolt of AD 69, Vellocatus replaces Venutius as royal consort and neither of these occurrences is included in both narratives. The *Annals* describes an attack from outside the kingdom – in the *Histories*, Cartimandua faces a combination of external assault and internal rebellion. The first major conflict is anticipated by the governor who sends cohorts and then a legion, whilst in the later troubles, Cartimandua is forced to ask for help and receives only auxiliary cavalry and infantry. Most importantly, Venutius is routed after his first attack on the kingdom, but having learnt his lesson, he succeeds in overthrowing his former wife on his second attempt: 'Venutius inherited the throne, and we the fighting' (Tacitus, *Histories*, 3.45).

Those who accept the plausibility of the 'flash-back' theory sometimes discount the idea of two rebellions because of the problem of the intervening years between events. If there was no reconciliation, then what was Venutius doing during those 12 or so years? Why did he not take

ANNALS AD 51-57	*REBELLION*	*HISTORIES* AD 69
Pro-Roman Venutius		Anti-Roman Venutius
Capture of Caratacus		Capture of Caratacus
Hostility between Royal couple		Hostility between Royal couple
Cartimandua captures Venutius' relatives		Vellocatus replaces Venutius as consort
Attack launched from outside the kingdom		External attack combined with internal uprising
Romans anticipated Venutius' attack		Cartimandua appealed for help
Legion and cohorts		Auxiliary infantry and cavalry
Venutius repelled		Queen rescued leaving Venutius in power

14 Braund's 'Flash-back' Theory   ▨ Original events   ▨ Flashback

advantage of the Boudican rebellion and why were the Brigantes so keen to support Venutius in revolt if the royal couple had been divorced all this time (Hanson & Campbell, 1986, 79)? These are pertinent questions that have already been answered. By keeping his relatives as hostages and persuading her Roman friends not to seek vengeance for the first rebellion, Cartimandua could have gained herself some time to make new alliances within the tribal federation. Cautiously waiting to see the outcome of Boudica's rebellion, Venutius took his time in replenishing his forces and gaining new support as the terrible repercussions that followed the south-eastern revolt persuaded the rival factions within the Brigantian alliance away from further resistance for a while. The tribal queen incensed her people by later marrying a Roman – this final straw coupled with the opportunity to act when Rome was preoccupied with infighting would explain the chronology of events as set out in the two narratives. Different rebellions, different forces involved, different outcomes.

THE NATURE OF IMPERIALISM

Tacitus breaks off his narrative of the civil wars in Rome in AD 69 to talk about the Brigantian rebellion. Resuming the story, the Emperor Vitellius held on to the purple by his fingertips as his rival, the popular Vespasian, drew supporters to him. Mucianus, the governor of Syria was one such ally and he led a strong force taken from the Syrian and Judaean legions in a march on Rome. The Danubian legions of Raetia and Moesia also hailed Vespasian as emperor and led by Primus, the commander of Legion VII, they invaded Italy, winning a great victory over the emperor's forces at the second Battle of Bedriacum (the first having occurred earlier in the year when Otho was defeated). They advanced on the capital and Vitellius was taken prisoner and put to death. Having sent his generals ahead to Italy, Vespasian was in Alexandria when he heard the news of Vitellius' downfall and execution (Suetonius, *Vespasian*, 7). He succeeded to the throne amid division in Rome and rebellion in Germany in the last few days of the year that had seen three other emperors come and go. However, despite the dangers open to all usurpers, that of perishing by the same violent means by which they ascended to their position, the Flavian dynasty which began with Vespasian's rule was to last for another 27 years, with its founder dying of natural causes in AD 79.

Empires predate the Romans by centuries and continue long after their influence waned. Our more recent examples of imperialism in the British Empire are said to reflect the experiences of Rome but is this a self-fulfilling prophecy? British rulers were classically schooled and brought up to believe in the glory of such a conquering force – in attempting to emulate the ancient state, did they repeat all of her examples instead of learning from her mistakes? The Indian Mutiny of 1857-8 saw an uprising against British rule in India, led by the sepoys or native soldiers. The expansion of the East India Company at the expense of the native princes was only one of the simmering tensions that were ignited into warfare. In containing the trouble, the British were said to have been aided by the loyalty of Sikhs in the Punjab and the compliance of the south. The sepoys and the Punjabi people were not friendly or in alliance and yet the latter have been accused of betraying their countrymen, before India even considered itself one nation (Singh, 1972). Atrocities were committed on both sides as civilians, women and children were killed – the British and Indian 'collaborators' were targeted by the rebels, unleashing a terrible and bloody retaliation once the mutiny was put down. This all sounds very familiar. However, if the model of Rome had not been followed, would the later civilisations have taken a similar path anyway in their ambitions for expansion?

Whether in reference to ancient Rome or colonial Britain, the same mistaken perceptions and emotive judgements can be made. In his article in the *BBC History Magazine* (January 2008, 32), Snook confronts the idea of 'native-bashing' and makes the excellent point that:

... an overly politically correct portrayal of Queen Victoria's enemies as helpless victims of imperialism serves only to demean the often sophisticated indigenous societies of the time. In military terms it belittles their intelligence, their fighting spirit and their capacity for a degree of guile as highly developed, if not more so, than that of their British opponents.

As with Rome's invasion of Britain, native resistance is often discounted because the final battle is lost, but many details are also often omitted to present a certain picture – there needs to be a villain in any historical scenario and recounting atrocities committed by both sides would lessen the dramatic impact of the story. On a personal level, it does not help our true understanding to victimise the defeated in this way. Knowing that the Boudican hordes may have committed bloody acts of their own does not detract from any sympathy we may feel for their original plight – we understand a warrior culture better in knowing that they did not passively allow themselves to be oppressed once the battle cry was sounded. In the same way, being aware of the abuses inherent in the Roman Empire does not stop us from admiring its strengths. Absolutes used to be for small children, but as the old boundaries are blurred with the flawed heroes shown in *Harry Potter* and other such gems, it seems that the comfort that is to be had from black and white judgements remains in our adult world. Interestingly, the history of the conquest of ancient Britain as told by Rome paints a much more flattering picture of the quality of native resistance than our modern accounts of colonial opposition. The former focused on making their victories seem greater by glorifying their opponents and the latter, in expressing a sense of guilt for the moral ramifications of violently annexing so many cultures, judging the past by current standards of acceptable behaviour.

THE FALL OF BRIGANTIA

The goddess Brigantia continued to be worshipped in the north of Britain until the early third century at least, as the Birrens relief (Fig. 5) was dedicated to her some time around the mid to late Severan period (Henig, 2007) and the inscriptions mentioned earlier confirm this approximate time frame. Venutius, sitting on the usurped throne of Brigantia did not have so lengthy a stay. If Cartimandua had been the 'living symbol' of the tribal goddess (Ziegler, 1999), then her overthrow was clearly not popular with the deity as her replacement lasted less than five years, ruling the territory in his own right.

After the initial euphoria of victory had settled down, he must have appreciated the precariousness of his position. Used to Cartimandua's influence with the Roman administration, the people would have wanted assurances of protection and the shadow of possible reprisals must have constantly followed him around. It has often been said that grass is always greener on the other side of the fence – having to control tribal factions squabbling over the spoils of the recent uprising and plotting their own attempts at gaining greater power, Venutius would have realised that the act of juggling alliances was made much more difficult without a sizeable bodyguard. Venutius was a military man – his strategies may have only taken him to the point of overthrowing his former wife and not included the running of the kingdom afterwards. He would not be able to rely on Roman subsidies or assistance in times of bad harvests, but having removed their hereditary queen, the Brigantes would still expect Venutius to assume her mantle of responsibility. As many ambitious individuals have found once they ousted someone in power, it is easy to be popular with the masses when someone else is making all the tough decisions.

Cartimandua's fate will be considered later, but neither she nor the governor, Vettius Bolanus, made an immediate attempt to retake the throne. The new king must have been very grateful for the unwarlike actions of the Roman official (Tacitus, *Agricola*, 8). If the Brigantian uprising ended at the close of AD 69 and Bolanus' successor took over early in AD 71, that gave him at least a year in power without serious conflict, or did it? Although we are indebted to Tacitus for his assessment of the governor's term, the poet Statius suggests an alternative version of events. In a letter addressed to Bolanus' son, Crispinus, we are told that his father took some armour 'from a British chief and this he did himself at the battle-call' (Statius, *The Silvae*, 5.2.149). This may just be poetic licence. Milman, in editing Gibbon's *The History of the Decline and Fall of the Roman Empire*, believes that the 'flattery and metaphor' inherent in Statius' description of Bolanus' British successes must be compared with his 'real character' as shown in Tacitus' *Agricola* 16 (Gibbon, 1845, Vol 2, Chapter XXV, Part V, n.119). However, Wolfson believes that both sources may be biased: 'The fact that Tacitus was closer to Agricola than Statius to Bolanus is more likely to raise doubts than inspire confidence in him as a source' (2002, Part 5). *Agricola* is the biography of one of Britain's most famous Roman governors written by a son-in-law who respected and loved him, whereas Statius and Crispinus were just thought to be friends, rather than being related. Agricola knew

Britain well, having served on Suetonius Paulinus' staff at the time of the Boudican rebellion. He also commanded Legion XX *Valeria* under the governorships of both Vettius Bolanus and his successor Petillius Cerealis and it is possible that Tacitus' unflattering portrayals of both men could have had their origins in an inherited familial attitude. The Roman author misses few chances to portray his relative in a positive light (acknowledging his 'affection' in *Agricola*, 3) and he has been seen consistently to lessen the achievements of Agricola's predecessors as governor of Britain (Hanson, 1987, 18). However, despite any bias, Agricola is said to have combined his military achievements with tactful administration, prudence and a certain sympathy for the provincials, exhibiting his skill as a tactician by leading the British people towards the 'attractions of peace' to gain their compliance (Tacitus, *Agricola*, 20-1; Richmond, 1944, 35, 43-4).

Thus, in examining Tacitus' description of Bolanus' term of office, Birley notes that any supposed inactivity would refer to the period in AD 69 when civil war still raged and that the governor could well have campaigned in the north for the rest of his time in Britain (Birley, 1976, 46). Petillius Cerealis is credited with fighting Venutius and the Brigantes between AD 71 and AD 74 and Agricola is known to have campaigned in Scotland, but as Wolfson proposes:

> Bolanus had possibly two campaigning seasons to deal with Venutius and the Brigantes, sufficient time for operations in southern Scotland, and may well deserve some of the credit which Tacitus gives to Cerealis, just as Cerealis deserves some of the credit given to Agricola. It would not suit Agricola's *curriculum vitae* to credit Bolanus with any initiatives.
>
> Wolfson, 2002, Part 5, n.325

If Venutius was the British king that Statius referred to, then he may only have had a few months of untroubled rule before having to defend his position, but if Tacitus was correct about Bolanus, Brigantia may have had peace for a little longer. This was only ever going to be a temporary state of being though. Rome had lost her major ally in the north, a buffer state that prevented the northern tribes from attacking and southern rebels from fleeing the province. Moreover, the Romans did not know Venutius' future plans – they may have feared that he would try to avenge his former defeat by attacking occupied southern territory whilst their numbers were depleted, as Legion XIV *Gemina* was recalled from Britain in AD 70.

Timing again proved crucial to the events that followed. Venutius was either extremely unlucky or cursed by the Brigantian gods, for in AD 71, the supposedly docile Vettius Bolanus was replaced by Petillius Cerealis, a seasoned and driven soldier. Again, unfortunately for the Brigantian leader, what motivated the new governor was a determination to crush any rebellion in expanding the province. He arrived in Britain having just put down the Batavian revolt led by Civilis in Germany. This was also the same Cerealis whose rescue mission to Colchester was foiled when a large number of his troops from Legion IX *Hispana* were ambushed and slaughtered by Boudica's army in AD 60-1. He and his cavalry escaped, but his tolerance of native resistance would not have been improved by such incidents.

With Venutius gaining the throne by force as Vespasian had done, their positions were similarly based on usurpation. However, although the emperor's position was born of the violence of civil war, he was quick to distance himself from these unpleasant events, focussing on restoring the peace, rebuilding the Empire and gaining the loyalty of the army and the people of Rome. As we have seen, Imperial expansion was a useful tool for new emperors wishing to build a reputation and Vespasian planned to utilise all the means at his disposal. Cartimandua had been forcibly removed from her throne and the protection she had given Imperial interests went with her – the Roman province was now open to attack from the north.

Both Vespasian and Venutius had violently taken their respective thrones, but what was *garum* for the Roman goose was certainly not sauce for the Brigantian gander. For those unfamiliar with Roman condiments, *garum* was a delightful fish sauce made by squishing the entrails of various seafood items. It was described by Pliny as being 'prepared from the intestines of fish and various parts which would otherwise be thrown away, macerated in salt; so that it is, in fact, the result of their putrefaction' (Pliny, *The Natural History*, 31.43). The Britons must have been overjoyed to add such a delicacy to their 'barbarian' diet and the desirability of Romano-British alliances must have been tested when the Roman guest presented a pot of that stuff to his native hostess.

Petillius Cerealis was determined to change the post-Boudican policy of fortification, rather than expansion, supported by his father-in-law, the Emperor Vespasian (Townend, 1961, 58-9). Bringing new troops to the province with him in the form of Legion II *Adiutrix* and thus returning the British contingent back to its original level, the governor's first priority was to make a direct strike against the Brigantes. His family seemed destined to be connected with the northern tribe as the Caesius Nasica who led the legion that defeated Venutius in the first Brigantian rebellion in the AD 50s was thought to be Petillius Cerealis' brother (Birley, 1973, 181). It must have been the ultimate slap in the face for

Venutius, to have the same family rob of him of victory, not once but twice. The commander was a man of immediate action – Tacitus should have been ecstatic, but he disliked the new governor and so now had someone else to criticise. Unable to lump him in with his inactive predecessors, the Roman author chose to focus on what he saw as Petillius Cerealis' incompetence, lack of caution and failure to preserve discipline in his posts prior to arriving in Britain (Birley, 1973, 183, 186). However, the commander must have been popular with his soldiers initially at least, as having had very limited opportunities for action in the years of 'peaceful recovery', they would have loved the chance to get back to fighting and plundering. Action also served the dual purpose of bringing discipline back to the army after the effects of the civil war by focusing any negative feelings on the enemy (Tacitus, *Annals*, 1.49) and showing 'the barbarians outside the Empire that Rome's strength was undiminished' (Richmond, 1944, 35).

If this new aggressive campaign did come on the back of Bolanus' attempt to conquer Brigantia, Venutius would not even have had a chance to enjoy his 'honeymoon period' as ruler. The days in exile with his own people free from the reprisals of his first attack on the kingdom must have seemed far away and infinitely preferable. However, if he was an accomplished military man from a warrior culture, the risk of death on the battlefield with the possibility of glory could have been the chance he had been waiting many years for. Such men cannot abide inactivity and given that he could have begun fighting the Romans almost immediately after the rebellion, it is most likely that he was out of the country in the years between his two attacks on Brigantia. By offering his skills to the troubled tribes abroad, he may have escaped the Roman reprisals that way and only returned when he knew another opportunity had presented itself in Brigantia. It could have been part of his agreement with Cartimandua that he leave the country – she held onto his relatives as hostages to ensure they did not cause any more trouble and may even have hoped that Venutius would die on some battlefield in Germany or Gaul and save her some trouble. If that was the case, she was to be disappointed. Continuing in combat would likely have 'kept his hand in' for when he came back to Britain and he may even have brought some new support with him. Hunting, fishing and sparring would have kept him fit, but there is no substitute for real fighting to keep the reflexes sharp. Free from the constraints of his powerful ex-wife, Venutius could finally follow his own inclinations. Whether a lapsed ally of Rome or her long-term enemy, there was no longer any doubt what his intentions were. He must have negotiated a settlement with many of the tribal groups and impressed upon them the necessity for unity in the face of this new and more powerful Roman threat.

With such obvious expansionist policies in place, it is clear that Rome was not going to return Cartimandua to the throne of Brigantia. As Claudius had done before him, Vespasian was keen to have a British victory to set the seal on his accession to the purple. During the tribal queen's rule, Rome had been content to help her police her borders, stepping in on several occasions to remove any serious threat to her throne. However, the instability surrounding Cartimandua's overthrow meant that the kingdom would be easier to rule directly – the Empire could not allow a known dissident to be in control of such a pivotal area for long. It is possible that the queen did not want to rule an occupied Brigantia – she had managed to keep its independence for what could have been almost 30 years with careful political manoeuvring and both she and Rome may have had other plans for her future. The Brigantes were to be punished for their uprising and this time they did not have a powerful voice to protect their interests – Cartimandua had been forced to leave her birthright behind and if she had been the goddess's representative, some of her people may have been uneasy about such an expulsion. In ancient British society, clear victory after battle may have been enough to justify such an action, but as Elizabeth I was to discover in condemning her cousin Mary, the removal of a hereditary queen was a serious matter.

The governor's advance into Brigantia was swift and decisive. Tacitus outlines the campaign in the following terms:

> Petilius Cerealis at once struck terror into their hearts by attacking the state of the Brigantes, which is said to be the most populous in the whole province. After a series of battles – some of them by no means bloodless – Petilius had overrun, if not actually conquered, the major part of their territory.
>
> Tacitus, *Agricola*, 17

On first reading, it may almost be assumed that the Roman author was feeling complimentary, but just when a pre-Agricolan governor seems surprisingly to emerge unscathed, we are hit with the aftertaste of negative suggestion. The above passage was preceded by an encouraging opening, as Tacitus talks of Vespasian ushering in a new period of administrative stability and military competence in Britain. Things are looking good so far. Petillius Cerealis frightens the Brigantes (Tacitus employs a touch of poetic licence here as Northerners are made of sterner stuff than that) and succeeds in his assault on their territory. This is not so wonderful for the native people, but is impressive work by the governor and his men. Tacitus, however, did not appear to think so. As Hanson points out, the Roman author manages to convey the impression of an incomplete triumph (Hanson, 1987, 39). For Petillius Cerealis there are no details forthcoming about the victory and no eloquent speeches given to either illustrious general before battle commences.

Considering that Venutius was supposed to have such a great military reputation and had beaten the Romans in overthrowing Cartimandua, the fact that Tacitus does not even mention his name, let alone his history, is very strange. It goes against the whole idea of praising Roman opponents to make the victory seem even more triumphant, especially when Venutius had a background of resistance to the Empire, just as Caratacus had done. There is no suggestion that the outcome of this campaign was unsatisfactory, as Petillius Cerealis had a successful career in Rome after finishing his term of office in Britain and Tacitus would have been sure to pounce on any hint of wrongdoing. Such minimal coverage therefore suggests that it is just another example of the Roman author playing down a governor's success. As already noted, Tacitus seemed to have disliked Petillius Cerealis and may have had valid reasons for doing so. However, it is likely that one of these reasons was probably that the man had had the temerity to rule Britain in a competent fashion, even extending the provincial boundaries before the golden age of Agricola was ushered in.

Thus with the possible bias of our source acknowledged, an examination of the chain of events leading to Roman victory in Brigantia can be attempted. Venutius would have expected an attack if he knew of the governor's military background, so he must have had a plan to counter the annexation of his sizeable lands. The key to successful British resistance thus far seemed to have been knowledge of the terrain and surprise attacks. Such guerrilla warfare removed the advantage to the Romans of pitched battle and enabled the rebels to attack before the deadly troop formations were employed. The fact that Tacitus describes a number of bloody encounters suggests that Venutius may have employed such tactics in defending Brigantia. The Boudican rebellion had shown what one big battle could do to a native force, while Caratacus' lengthy 'hit and run' strategy had allowed him to exploit every chance of weakening the Roman advance. The Catuvellaunian rebel had fought and retreated through Wales over a number of years, and only failed when he ran out of land to move back to and decided to engage his enemies in a face-to-face battle. Venutius had a large expanse of Brigantian land to utilise – much of it was remote high ground that would have put Petillius Cerealis' forces at a serious disadvantage.

We do not know how many fought on either side, but if the rebel leader could tie up the Romans in a series of skirmishes, he could bide more time and gain even more followers. His main advantage would have been that in pulling back northwards, he was likely heading in the direction of his own people. This could have been why Tacitus scathingly referred to the governor overrunning rather than conquering much of Brigantia, as the rebels may have continually retreated rather than being decisively crushed. Venutius may have been happy to leave Stanwick and his former wife's strongholds to her Roman friends, especially as we do not know where he was based prior to the governor's advance. As shown earlier and on current evidence, it is unlikely that the rebels occupied the former Brigantian capital anyway – it would have been hard to defend from any invading force and with its high-status trappings long gone, the settlement which had been designed to impress probably symbolised a former life that was best forgotten. The further north Venutius marched, the more sympathisers he may have gathered, especially as he reached the Scottish border. Hind mentions the name of a place near Newstead in the Lowlands of Scotland known as *Venution* and proposes that it could have been linked in some way to the Brigantian leader (Hind, 1977, 230). Birley supports the idea of a pursuit northwards (1973, 190) and later elaborates on the theme, suggesting that as Venutius was joined by supporters from the Lowlands in his fight against Cartimandua, then *Venutio* (as he refers to it) could possibly be so-named in remembrance of a final anonymous battle with Rome (Birley, 1976, 45-6).

That, of course, assumes that there was a final battle. It is entirely possible that a decisive showdown was never achieved and could have been one of the reasons for Tacitus' griping. If Venutius was not captured or killed in battle, then it may not have been seen as a decisive victory and yet if that had been the case, Tacitus would surely have emphasised it in his narrative. Had Venutius died in the process of retreat, either of natural causes or after being wounded say, then the Romans could not boast of his final defeat – another famous rebel, like Caratacus or Boudica, would have apparently evaded Roman punishment. The Brigantian leader's age is unknown, but if he had married Cartimandua before the Roman invasion of AD 43 and he was older than his bride, then he may have been somewhere in his fifties or older. The death of Venutius may have finished the Romans' job for them if support had melted away without a charismatic leader to keep the fight going, just as Dio described in his account of the Boudican rebellion.

This rebel's demise could not be written off as a suicide in the sources, however – he had not lost a major engagement so there was no reason for him to kill himself, honourably or otherwise. As it was, he just disappeared from the historical narrative and we do not know what happened to him. His plan may have been to continue leading the Romans on a scenic tour of Northern Britain until they ran out of men, having been picked off one ambush at a time or until Petillius Cerealis was replaced by someone less fond of outdoor chases. Another power shift in Rome could have changed events if the legions were again withdrawn to fight elsewhere. All Venutius had to do was keep his army reasonable mobile, attacking and raiding where he could, and not fall prey to the desire for all-out conflict. It may have been a tempting possibility for men used to battling their enemies, but not a prudent one.

For a man so seasoned in rebellion and with the possibility of many more years and new areas of support to come, he is unlikely to have just given up the struggle. He had waited many years to have the chance to fight on his own terms and even when conclusively beaten in the first Brigantian rebellion, he still returned to the fray. Succumbing to an illness or an infected wound, his body could have been given a great warrior's send-off and the Romans would have been none the wiser. They would have had to look harder for resistance and given that the rebels could have been moving into areas outside Brigantia, they could have just declared the campaign a victory. If Venutius had died towards the end of the governor's term, he would have ruled Brigantia for five years at most, although it was likely to have been a much shorter reign. Popular with his people, he may even have been respected by his enemies. He had not fled to be hounded the rest of his days, but had made several stands against Rome once his marriage had ended. The region was certainly no longer considered a threat by the time of Petillius Cerealis' successor, Julius Frontinus, who concentrated his efforts on conquering the fiery Silures in Wales when he took his post as governor of Britain in AD 74. It was not until the mighty Agricola arrived four years later that the far north became a major focus once more.

5

The Queen, the Woman, the Invention

The ancient historical narratives of Tacitus and Dio hold much more value than merely informing the contemporary reader of the various dates and places an event occurred. They are a barometer of their time, measuring the pressure of conformity to the norms of their society, and allowing us to assess the possible political and moral climate of Imperial Rome. Regardless of the personal biases of the respective authors, these works were written to please a certain type of audience and so reflect the popular mentality and ideals prevalent in their world. Women were acknowledged as playing a small number of limited roles in the events that shaped and also shook an Empire, but their true part in the history that was recorded for posterity peeks out from behind the often unflattering stereotypical images they were given by the sources.

Cartimandua has not been treated any better by modern scholars, however. The words of the Roman authors have been repeated verbatim in many academic texts without careful examination and in isolation from any other pertinent material. Her ancient image has not been challenged and just like their predecessors, some contemporary historians have perpetuated the tired myth of the Brigantian barbarian queen because it is easier to copy than to question. Therefore, Cartimandua remains the adulterous betrayer of British royal men, the prone figures of Venutius and Caratacus forming the stepping stones towards the realisation of the queen's materialistic ambitions. Such fanciful notions seem almost laughable when formed in this language but the ideas behind this representation are just as absurd. Unlike the old parlour game of Chinese Whispers, the information murmured into many sets of ears has not changed for almost 2000 years. What began as a Roman dramatised caricature of a British hereditary queen all that time ago is now accepted as gospel fact, quoted and re-quoted without a thought for the image it portrays. Tacitus and Dio would probably be very amused to learn that the historical propaganda they devised to entertain a conquering nation is now the only accepted portrayal of a native queen in the country that Rome invaded. However, Cartimandua is not the only female ruler to be dealt with in this fashion. The images we have of Cleopatra and Boudica, Berenice of Cilicia and Elizabeth I have all been shaped by the attitudes and biases of a number of writers, translators and social commentators over many centuries.

PERCEPTIONS OF FEMININE INFLUENCE

... Did Celtic women have a role in Celtic society which made their contemporaries in Greece and Rome appear primitive?

Berresford Ellis, 1998, 87

For thousands of years, many religions existed that worshipped a female creator, the mother goddess. The ancient Britons of the Brigantes and Iceni tribes were protected by Brigantia and Andraste, their tribal deities and even today, many modern pagans worship a feminine divine being. Unfortunately, much of the evidence which would allow us to explore these historical faiths is now gone, destroyed by the Catholic Church in an attempt to abolish paganism. The Romans saw themselves as civilised and enlightened, but in religious terms, they were classed in the same light as their barbarian contemporaries. Jones cites Clark in describing how the sixth-century Pope Gregory the Great 'tried to suppress the works of Cicero and is said to have burnt all the manuscripts of Livy he could lay hands on' (Jones & Ereira, 2006, 31; Clark, 1921). Maybe this is why so much of Tacitus' work did not survive. Many of the ancient sources we know about came from books copied in the Irish monasteries, by those who wanted to preserve knowledge from various faiths. To compound the problem:

... most of the available information in both archaeology and ancient religious history was compiled and discussed by male authors. The overwhelming prevalence of male scholars, and the fact that nearly all archaeologists, historians and theologians of both sexes were raised in societies that embrace the male-oriented religions of Judaism or Christianity, appear to influence heavily what was included and expanded upon and what was considered to be minor and hardly worth mentioning.

Stone, 1976, xviii

Women in classical antiquity seem to have been given extreme parts to play, with opposites in morality, freedom and influence providing no happy medium. This polarity is reflected in the excellent title of Pomeroy's book, *Goddesses, whores, wives and slaves* (1976). She makes the point that the preference for political, intellectual and military history has often hidden the experiences of those people who were excluded by gender or background from participation in those spheres of their societies (Pomeroy, 1976, ix). Empresses and queens were the exception and the women we have the most evidence of, but their experiences were hardly representative of their sex as a whole.

It is interesting how disapproval is often cyclical – the Greeks considered anyone who was not Greek to be a barbarian and for all their enlightened thinking, their women were even less liberated in a social and cultural setting than the moral Roman matrons. The Romans took exception to this snobbery and they were more fluid in their societal divisions, yet they considered the people of the provinces to be largely barbarian. Women outside the Empire had more rights, freedom and open political power than their Italian contemporaries, and may have considered their restricted female role to be archaic. There was certainly a difference in outlook when it came to morality. The Empress Julia Domna had obviously believed the urban myth that British women frequently slept with men other than their husbands – no doubt inspired by Julius Caesar's description that 'ten and even twelve have wives common to them, and particularly brothers among brothers, and parents among their children' (Caesar, *Gallic War*, 5.14). She rather rudely asked the wife of the Caledonian chieftain, Argentocoxus, about 'the free intercourse of her sex with men in Britain' and was put down with the response that:

> We fulfil the demands of nature in a much better way than do you Roman women; for we consort openly with the best men, whereas you let yourselves be debauched in secret by the vilest.
>
> Cassius Dio, *Roman History*, 77.16.5

The empress was rumoured to have had a dubious personal life (Allason-Jones, 2005, 25) and if this was true, her hypocritical question may have been the result of her envy of the freedom enjoyed by British women. Unfortunately, we do not have any surviving British or Roman accounts written by women, but modern scholars like Lindsay Allason-Jones and Eve D'Ambra have utilised a variety of sources, examining inscriptions, letters, curse tablets, writing tablets, coins, art and burial evidence in an attempt to build a picture of the lives of women in pagan antiquity.

Rome and Greece propitiated many powerful goddesses and yet their attitude to ordinary female influence was very different, which may explain their fascination with 'barbarian queens'. Rome itself was always referred to in the feminine, so it could be that in their culture, to inspire such loyalty, fear and worship, the powerful female had to be unreachable, distant and able to be put on a pedestal. Elizabeth I famously never took a husband as she considered herself wedded to England and the 'Virgin Queen' remained an object of devotion and loyalty despite her refusal to provide her kingdom with an heir. Roman men were happy to die for their Empire and their goddesses, and the hint of approachability in their objects of reverence would have shattered such perceptions. The Vestal Virgins had much power, privilege and influence in ancient Rome as long as they stayed, or appeared to remain, chaste and uncorrupted. Queens like Cartimandua would have held a fascination for the Roman audience as their 'otherness' centred around the fact that they were female barbarians who ruled in their own right. In describing Cleopatra, Hughes-Hallett notes that 'even in her lifetime her legend was already shaped by the two overlapping chauvinisms of race and sex, for in a man's world every woman is a foreigner' (Hughes-Hallett, 2006, 15), but she could have been talking about any powerful barbarian queen.

Cartimandua's 'otherness' could also have been enhanced by the reputation her people had in Rome. We have seen that Seneca was Nero's tutor and the lender of large sums to Britain prior to the Boudican rebellion, but he was also a celebrated philosopher who turned his hand to satire on one occasion to describe the Emperor Claudius. The resulting *Apocolocyntosis*, written early in Nero's reign, distinguished between the Britons and the Brigantes, as we noted earlier, but it also showed how the latter were perceived in Rome at that time. Seneca talks of the Brigantes being ordered to submit to Roman authority (*Apocolocyntosis*, 12.11-15), but although part of an ironic work, Braund suggests that the tribe had gained a reputation for being difficult and that this reference 'indicates that the Brigantes were far from being under Roman control c. AD 54' (Braund, 1996, 125). This attitude to the northern tribe would also support the 'two rebellions' theory as the minor skirmish put down by Scapula in AD 48 would not have been enough to warrant such a mention in Rome. However, the first Brigantian uprising in the AD 50s would have been, especially as Cartimandua would have been known for her part in Caratacus' capture a few years earlier.

BOUDICA OF THE ICENI

The ancient sources distrusted and disapproved of female rulers, as did their audience. Female political competence and loyalty was not an issue – Berenice aided Vespasian in his path to the Imperial throne and Cartimandua's support helped the Romans to establish and extend their British province. However, all such independent queens were frowned upon and were made into a recognisable stereotype. Their autonomy was enough to inspire objection, as there was no male superior to guide their behaviour. If their queenly loyalties could not be questioned then their morals were to be so judged; if their morals were unimpeachable, then the women would be criticised for exhibiting unfeminine traits, although their very sovereignty took them out of the traditional roles expected of Roman women. In the set speech given to Boudica by Dio, she mentions Nitocris, Semiramis, Messalina and Agrippina (*Roman History*, 62.6.2-3): two famous barbarian queens and two empress wives of Claudius, although infamous would be a better word.

We have seen that powerful empresses and queens were often categorised as either masculine or sexually improper and here Dio follows the trend, rather thoroughly including an even number of Roman and foreign royals and an equal split of undesirable qualities. Messalina and the Syrian Semiramis were notorious for their sexual excesses, whilst the Egyptian Nitocris (Herodotus, *The Histories*, 2.100.1) and Agrippina acted like men in gaining bloody vengeance and aspiring to supreme power respectively. They were all examples of female rulers notorious for their links to murder, lust, ambition and power and coincidentally not one of them died a natural death, obviously serving as a cautionary tale for any woman who desired to step outside the acceptable boundaries set for her in Roman society. Collingridge (2005, 239) explains that 'although at face value, Boudica is raised up to the pantheon of the known-world's hall of fame for queens, the list of women rulers would do little to enhance her reputation; to Dio's educated Roman audience, she would be damned by association'.

It seems strange that Dio would link the virtuous Boudica to queens with dubious sexual morals, but unlike Tacitus, he never mentions her marital status, motherhood or the abuses that are said to have triggered the rebellion. His Boudica is a horrible masculine figure who finds 'an excuse for war' (Dio, *Roman History*, 62.2.1) in financial concerns and is only stopped from fighting by her sudden death. A Roman audience would sympathise with a royal widow and mother being severely abused by social inferiors as her household was ravaged by slaves, despite her barbarian origins, and the Boudica Tacitus describes in the *Annals* is worthy of such sentiment. In portraying Boudica as a royal woman, rather than a queen, she is not burdened with the negative stereotypical characteristics associated with the latter position and in fighting for a just cause and for values that Rome used to prize, her bravery may be admired despite her gender (Braund, 1996, 132, 135). However, she cannot be the hero of the piece, so as the rebellion unfolds Suetonius Paulinus returns Rome to the higher moral ground – Tacitus shows the rational commander defeating the misguided barbarians whose futile gesture in resisting Rome was doomed to failure.

Both Tacitus and Dio used Boudica's example to make points to their audiences, but they differed in their approach in doing so. In portraying her first as a woman, a mother and wife, Tacitus then questions her actions as a queen, whilst Dio's warlike monarch, devoid of a sympathetic family situation, is automatically seen as less of a woman:

> In both Tacitus and Dio, Boudica embodies issues of gender and power. Dio's Boudica is not Tacitus' Cartimandua but she has much in common with her. She is different because she is not inspired by illicit sex and because she seems to have a capacity to rule beyond that of Cartimandua's unstable regime. However, she is a very masculine woman, who therefore and almost paradoxically is seen as prone to promiscuity, for such is her power and the maleness of her potential.
>
> Braund, 1996, 145

Thus, those women in command are linked with sexual impropriety by virtue of their rule, rather than their personal conduct. Boudica was never shown to be anything less than modest, so juxtaposition with women of questionable morals must suffice; however, Cartimandua had the reputation of a faithless wife. Just as Boudica is contrasted with the governor who defeated her in dramatic opposition, she is held up as the moral superior of the hereditary queen who chose a different relationship with Rome. Yet as we have already seen, Cartimandua did not commit adultery. She had been divorced for more than a decade by the time she remarried – hardly the actions of an immoral woman.

The description of Vellocatus in Tacitus' *Histories* (3.45) has been translated as 'lover' by Wellesley (1995) and Levene (1997), and 'adulterer' by Church and Brodribb (1942). The Roman author may well have originally thought that an affair occurred when he wrote the earlier book, but he clearly had more information for his narrative in the prequel, the *Annals*, as he describes the divorce and hostilities leading to the first Brigantian revolt in the AD 50s. The point of the *Histories'* slant could have been meant to serve as a topical cautionary tale, warning Roman women of the consequences of such behaviour – Cartimandua had an affair and this led to her losing her kingdom. In Rome, if a woman was proved to have committed adultery, she and her lover were exiled to separate islands and she lost half her dowry and a third of her property. Cartimandua was an unmarried adulteress and an unpatriotic betrayer of her countryman before Britain was a united kingdom – it may be wondered why Tacitus did not go with 'masculine' angle, as it would have at least had a chance of looking credible. Cartimandua was loyal to Rome, protected her lands from invasion and made the mistake of angering her people in her choice of husband.

Tacitus cannot judge Cartimandua as a queen for she was a staunch Roman ally, so he must focus on her faults as a woman ruling her people, but even then he does not make a convincing case. A Brigantian historian writing at the time of these events may well have been able to portray Cartimandua in a terrible light – she discounted the wishes of her subjects, divorced one of their tribal leaders, married a Roman and allowed foreign forces to keep her on the throne. However, to a Roman audience her only fault should have been her sovereignty as a barbarian queen, although there may have been some opposition to her marriage to Vellocatus. Through testing times, Cartimandua had maintained her friendship with the Empire, protected their expansion, captured and handed over a dangerous rebel and distanced herself from her former husband once she saw him as a threat to the security of her kingdom which was also so important to Roman concerns. Tacitus describes the handing over of Caratacus in critical tones (*Annals*, 12.36) and the Roman audience is encouraged to think ill of the queen who captured one of their enemies. However, the Roman author describes a very similar circumstance when Eunones, king of the Aorsi, surrenders the rebel ruler Mithridates to Rome (Tacitus, *Annals*, 12.15-21) – another example of his 'self-imitation' and also a chance for Tacitus to display his hostility to Cartimandua and all independent queens, for though she is censured, Eunones is seen to act correctly (Braund, 1996, 128-9). This antagonism is also displayed in his description of the first Brigantian rebellion, but this time he plainly makes Cartimandua's role as a queen an issue when he voices her adversaries' supposed worries of being degraded by female dominion (Tacitus, *Annals*, 12.40).

BERENICE OF CILICIA

Caratacus and Venutius are praised by Tacitus, and Cartimandua is seen to be to blame for her treatment of both of them. If she had not arrested the Catuvellaunian rebel, she would have been seen as a weak woman who did not honour her political alliances, preferring to honour a bond with her fellow Britons and ruling compassionately rather than shrewdly. Although her former husband is described as aggressive and detesting Rome, it is the fact that Venutius is 'goaded to fury' by his fight with Cartimandua which causes the trouble (Tacitus, *Histories*, 3.45). However unfair her treatment in the sources may have been, she was not the only queen who was loyal to Rome and whose personal relationships caused public disapproval.

During the Jewish War in the late AD 60s, Vespasian was sent to deal with the trouble in Berenice of Cilicia's lands. When civil war followed in Rome, the Judaean queen used her power and wealth to support his bid for the Imperial throne – she was in love with his son, Titus, who was said to have 'nursed a notorious passion' for her in return (Suetonius, *Titus*, 7). He brought her back to Rome where they lived together in the palace, as 'she expected to marry him and was already behaving in every respect as if she were his wife' (Dio, *Roman History*, 66.15.3-4). However, a barbarian queen 10 years Titus' senior was never going to be acceptable to the Roman people as empress material, so when his father died and he took the throne, Berenice was sent away, 'which was painful for both of them' (Suetonius, *Titus*, 7).

Of course, as a queen we know all of this about her private life and yet very little about her reign. Tacitus is surprisingly complimentary about Berenice, stating that 'she was in her best years and at the height of her beauty, while even the elderly Vespasian appreciated her generosity' (Tacitus, *Histories*, 2.81). However, this comment relates to the year AD 69 before she had gone to Rome and been promised marriage by Titus – one suspects that her qualities may have diminished in his account of these events, but this part of his work is missing. As with Boudica in the *Annals*, as a woman she may be admired, but her reign is not discussed in the fragments that survive. The Jewish historian, Josephus, relates that Berenice had a number of failed marriages during the early AD 40s and he also hints of an incestuous relationship with her brother (*The Antiquities of the Jews*, 19.5.1, 19.9.1, 20.7.3), a rumour which is repeated in Juvenal's famous *Satire 6*. Tacitus' narrative of this earlier period does not survive either, so we are left with the impression that there is at least one queen who is not portrayed with total disapproval.

CLEOPATRA OF EGYPT

Berenice's relationship with Titus was doomed – the idea of another Roman leader being ensnared by a barbarian queen must have caused panic in Rome, even though more than a century had passed since Cleopatra's relationship with Mark Anthony. The two queens were compared, as both were thought to have had aspirations of becoming Empress of Rome. Berenice certainly had been living in the palace with Titus and there is every possibility that he would have married her if his people had not strenuously objected. However, Cleopatra's relationships with Julius Caesar and Mark Anthony were primarily based on the political advantages that could be gained by both parties, whatever feelings may also have been involved. The Judaean queen used her wealth and influence to help Titus' father to the throne, but the Queen of Egypt demanded payment for her support. Both Caesar (*c.*48 BC) and Anthony (*c.*41 BC) needed money when they went to Cleopatra in Egypt – she wanted protection from her enemies, to rule alone and to expand the wealth and influence of her realm. Her claim to Roman rule was through her son, Caesarion, but he was never publicly acknowledged by Julius Caesar and it has never been proven if he really was the father.

Cartimandua and Cleopatra were hereditary queens who owed their continued success to their ties with Rome. Although the latter had personal relationships with the Roman men who guaranteed her protection, both queens were shrewd enough to appreciate when they were in a strong position and negotiated accordingly. It has been suggested that Cartimandua's marriage to Venutius could have been a dynastic alliance designed to cement Brigantian tribal relations and Vellocatus may have been able to protect her from the troubles in her realm. Brigantia was integral to the success of Rome's conquest plans and its security became tied up with Cartimandua's own – she remained on the throne, defended by Roman arms against internal and external unrest. Cleopatra had several rivals for her throne who were killed as the price of her funding Roman military expeditions – for in controlling the grain shipments to Rome and by continually increasing her country's legendary wealth, she was often in a position to dictate terms with her political allies. However, unlike Egypt, Brigantia was never occupied whilst Cartimandua was queen.

These women showed considerable skill in the business of governing their respective lands, with their reigns lasting for more than 20 years (possibly nearer 30 for the British queen). Cleopatra was known to have been an efficient administrator as:

... under her management the economy was strong, despite the massive debts incurred by her father, and despite Julius Caesar's having so ruthlessly milked the country to pay for his own civil wars. By the end of her reign Egypt was once again rich enough for Cleopatra to be able to pay and provision Anthony's army and to build a fleet to rival Rome's, and this vast expenditure on warfare seems scarcely to have dented her country's wealth.

Hughes-Hallett, 2006, 38-9

Her people never rose up in revolt against her – this could have been due to the fact that Roman legions maintained an active presence in Egypt, but as the British experience showed, if the native people are unhappy, they will rebel even if soldiers are close by. It is unlikely that the native Egyptians would have objected to their queen's alliance with foreign powers however, as she was not of ancient Egyptian blood – her family had Greek origins and had maintained their Hellenistic heritage despite their people's culture. Cleopatra was reputed, however, to be the first of her dynastic line in their 300-year reign in Egypt to embrace the religion and language of her subjects (Plutarch, *Life of Anthony*, 27) and in returning their land to prosperity, she showed herself to be a capable and dedicated ruler. Wheeler (1954, 19) mentions the idea that Cartimandua could have been a Belgic princess or from one of the southern tribes of Britain for:

> ... the Cartimandua-Venutius impasse is more easily intelligible if Cartimandua be regarded as an exile from the southern lands of cakes and wine, married incompatibly to a skin-clad rancher of the north, and thoroughly tired of unmitigated mutton.

Wonderfully vivid as this image is, it alas does not connect with Tacitus' description (*Annals*, 12.40), as in mentioning that Venutius was a Brigantian, he follows with the statement that he married 'the' tribal queen and not 'a' tribal queen. It would also not explain why the Brigantes rose up in mortification when their queen chose her new husband – if she had not been one of them, it would have been unlikely to have caused such a scandal. Cleopatra inherited her father's problems and yet she managed to strengthen the Egyptian economy through prudent administration and profitable foreign arrangements. If Cartimandua's predecessors had ruled the tribal federation in Brigantia, they could have been reasonably affluent, but it took their female replacement to bring the Brigantes the benefits of Roman gratitude. The huge and prestigious earthworks at Stanwick were erected in her reign and the settlement was known to have been at its most prosperous under Cartimandua's control.

Both queens had to risk the fortunes of their realms on their diplomatic choice of ally and both of them chose wisely at the time. Cartimandua maintained her alliance with Rome despite the threats of rebellions led by Caratacus and Boudica, and Cleopatra cautiously backed Octavian (who was to become the Emperor Augustus) and Anthony, rather than giving Brutus and Cassius, two of the men who assassinated Julius Caesar, the help they requested. These women were also similarly accused of treachery – Cartimandua and her 'betrayal' of Caratacus, and Cleopatra and her 'betrayal' of Anthony by deserting him at the Battle of Actium. The former charge has been shown to be false already, as the latter will also be. Anthony had effectively shared the rule of the Empire with Octavian after Caesar's murder, but hostile relations between them led to war. In 31 BC, Cleopatra and Anthony were trapped by Octavian's advance and their main concern was getting their treasure away from the conflict, thus giving them the funds that would enable them to fight again. Octavian needed this treasure to pay his troops – yet another Roman leader who relied on the wealth of the Egyptian royal coffers. When sails were loaded on Cleopatra's flagship at Actium, it was assumed that she planned to leave the battle – this was correct, but only so that they could support their continued resistance together as agreed, rather than because of a cowardly act (Hughes-Hallett, 2006, 46). Accusations of impropriety (usually sexual), against a strong female ruler who could not be greatly faulted in matters of state, were common. In attempting to reduce them merely to women, who ruled emotionally and not rationally, those threatened by their power sought to diminish their achievements. Cleopatra, Cartimandua and even Elizabeth I were all accused of immorality in their private lives because their competent behaviour as queen defied the boundaries that the male world had set for them.

Cleopatra's suicide is well known and part of her legend, and it is entirely possible that Tacitus' description of Boudica's death reflects the events of the Queen of Egypt's demise. Like Boudica, Cleopatra wished to avoid the humiliation of being paraded through the streets of Rome and it was said that Octavian was so desperate to keep the queen alive that he 'actually summoned Psyllian snake-charmers to suck the poison from her self-inflicted wound' (Suetonius, *Augustus*, 17). However, modern sources suggest slightly different behaviour. Octavian may have wished to be rid of such a persuasive foe and although Cleopatra is likely to have committed suicide anyway, he may have spread the rumour of her impending fate in order to ensure that she took her own life, and left her unguarded to allow her to do so (Hughes-Hallett, 2006, 49). It is not known whether Boudica took poison or died of an illness as Dio proposed – both accounts may be incorrect, but they at least give us something to work on. Berenice disappeared from the sources once she left Rome so we know nothing of the manner of her death and as we shall see, Cartimandua's fate is also a mystery. Thus, Cleopatra is the only barbarian queen where the sources agree about her death and she lived a century before our other examples. However, as she was Greek and not Egyptian, would she have been considered to be a foreign queen rather than a barbarian one? Either way, this issue is unlikely to have affected the opinion of her in Rome.

CARTIMANDUA'S FATE

Many historians dislike speculation, preferring to rely on the facts that they can prove, but a story must have an ending. There is no source material to question concerning Cartimandua's fate and so the only alternative is to follow the path taken so far in examining the possibilities and deciding on the most likely scenario. Braund (1984b, 5) outlines Reed's suggestion (1977, 41-3) that Cartimandua was to be housed at a purpose-built protected residence in Chester, but that the building was abandoned in AD 79 when the 'aged' tribal queen died. However, he then points out several flaws in this argument. Cartimandua was rescued by the Roman auxiliaries in AD 69, but the construction of this dwelling did not begin until at least five years after that, leaving a considerable time lag between the two events. If she was so old, it makes no sense to start building a dwelling for her after so long a delay – it would surely have been better to find her suitable existing accommodation. Reed considers Cartimandua to be elderly, but we do not know when she was born.

Supposing, as we did earlier, that the Brigantian queen was 20 at the time of the invasion in AD 43, this would mean that she was only just in her fifties by the time they would have begun building the new residence – she may have been older than that, but she could also conceivably have been younger. A woman of this age is hardly to be considered geriatric even by ancient standards and Tacitus described Queen Berenice as at her most beautiful in her forties. Age speculation aside, Braund believes there to be no connection between the Brigantian queen and the building as the fragmentary inscriptional evidence relied upon in this theory has been misinterpreted (1984b, 6, n.20).

If Cartimandua was going to be reinstated on the throne of Brigantia, it would have made sense to keep her protected somewhere near her territorial borders, as we do not know what new arrangements were made after order was restored in the AD 70s. There is no suggestion that this was ever an option, however, and this would surely have been mentioned in Tacitus' *Agricola*. With Rome having had to provide military aid on several occasions, once she was ousted annexation was inevitable and as mentioned earlier, Cartimandua may not have wanted to rule an occupied territory. Remaining in Brigantian lands would have left her too much of a target for Venutius to capture, so it would have made sense for her to begin a new life away from her tribal home. She could have died soon after the revolt, but if this had happened, Tacitus would no doubt have mentioned the event in some dramatic fashion. Had she been a warrior, there is scope for an honourable suicide, but we cannot have our only two British queens dying in the same way and anyway, Cartimandua had everything to live for – a new husband and the gratitude of Rome for her many years of support. In a world of invasion, rebellion and conflict, she had ruled her people for almost 30 years and apart from the two major revolts begun by her disgruntled ex-husband, she had had many years of peace in her unoccupied lands.

It is unlikely that she would have lived in another part of Britain as tribal relations were fractious at the best of times and military settlements would not have been the most congenial places for a displaced royal. Any living family she had may well have escaped Brigantia with her, rather than risk the treatment that Venutius and his victorious rebels would surely have dished out. However, a familial relationship does not guarantee loyalty or approval – her relatives could equally have remained in their tribal home supporting their former son-in-law. We do not know if she ever became a mother but Tacitus is likely to have mentioned any grown-up children, as they would have had an impact on the succession and the hostilities that erupted between Venutius and Cartimandua. A childless marriage would have been cause for friction in a time when ancestors were so important, and either one of them could have been infertile. However, if the queen had begun a relationship with Vellocatus after her divorce and conceived a child, this would further explain Venutius' hatred and the people's horror at the idea of having a half-Roman successor to the Brigantian throne.

Married to a Roman, most likely a Roman citizen herself and having been a loyal ally for many years, there was only one place to go. Cartimandua may have visited Rome before, but Vellocatus would have had family and connections there, and she may even have received a warm welcome

– whether she stayed there is another matter entirely. Braund (1988, 86-7) describes how 'to offer refuge to kings in flight from their kingdoms was to add still further to imperial prestige' and as a queen, she would have had even more interest. Cartimandua's presence in Rome could also have been seen as a diplomatic advantage. Tacitus describes how the Emperor Tiberius encouraged the flight of the friendly, defeated Germanic king, Maroboduus, to the capital and then portrayed the incident in the Senate as if he had saved Rome from a dangerous enemy by keeping the monarch in exile (Tacitus, *Annals*, 2.63). Cartimandua would never have been seen as an enemy, but her escape was evidence of the ferocity of the Venutian assault, making the annexation of Brigantia seem even more of a triumph in Rome. The tribal queen is likely to have spent her remaining days settled comfortably in a privileged life in Italy somewhere – she was not the first exiled British royal to do so, as both Adminius and Verica could well have remained there. If Caratacus was still alive, then they would no doubt have been kept apart, but had he been the great leader that his reputation suggests, he would have realised that Cartimandua was merely protecting her throne and her diplomatic position.

Cartimandua repeatedly risked the wrath of her people because of her decision to ally the kingdom with Rome, so she must have seen some merit in this path, other than protection from her enemies. She saw the future of her realm linked to diplomacy and not warfare – expanding her connections meant new avenues of trade for Brigantian goods, new opportunities for increasing her territory's wealth and a better life for her people. The Brigantes had not been abused or enslaved, she had seen how people who resisted Rome were treated and it made no sense for a queen who wished her people to prosper to stand in the way of the Imperial steamroller.

Boudica has been accused of leading her people to their deaths in a futile gesture because nothing changed after she was gone. However, that is the risk that every leader takes when they commit their forces to battle. Defeat is often followed by criticism from a number of armchair strategists, but they are not in the position of making life and death choices. Her brave stand was a gamble but Boudica might just as easily have won the battle. The Romans could have decided to withdraw from the province and we would be celebrating this Independence Day in modern times just as the French and Americans do with their own. Boudica and her army were fighting for a multitude of reasons, some of them noble and others possibly less so, but they fought because they could and because they had been given no choice if they wished to retain any vestiges of honour. However her relationship with Rome began, Boudica could have been David to Rome's Goliath – instead she stood up to a bully and lost. Britain has always valued the effort rather than the success of a venture and it is probably one of the reasons that she has remained so popular. To say that her resistance to Rome was pointless is to ignore the decision that each person who died on the battlefield made in following her – they were not forced, but chose to die at a time, in a manner and for a cause they believed in. Even if they lost, which they clearly did not expect to do, to them it was a glorious and noble end, worthy of songs and stories to be told by their descendants. They did not fade away as slaves, beaten down by constant abuse, but wearing their symbols of valour, hearing their war horns and the cries of their tribal fellows.

However, just as Boudica took the steps she believed were right in leading her people, so did Cartimandua in doing what she thought was best for the Brigantes in the circumstances. Whether the Romans were right to invade, that is what they did and as the leader of her people, she dealt with the turn of events. She was pro-Roman in her diplomatic stance, but not anti-Brigantian by choosing such a path. There were elements in her kingdom that were resistant to change, just as there are in our society today. The Brigantian queen is judged by modern values but with no basis for comparison – our country has not been invaded in living memory and so we do not know how our own society would react to such an event. However, a contemporary attack on a united country is a very different experience to the one faced by the ancient Britons during the conquest of their independent tribal lands. If her kingdom had not been so pivotal to Roman plans, Cartimandua may well have had to deal with the possibility of occupation and the resulting tensions that that would have brought, and history would have been different. As it was, she was ambitious and adept at political manoeuvring and she was a very successful queen.

Rome may have conquered Cartimandua's country, but it never treated her badly. She was a native woman thriving in a man's world and she had managed it in a civilised fashion, using force to put down trouble but without the need for all-out war. Cartimandua had a grudging respect from Rome for her accomplishments, although they would not have liked the fact that she was a woman ruling alone. She succeeded where Boudica had failed in beating Rome at their own game – that of power and influence – and her strength was that she did not attempt to push too far. She did not extend her boundaries or ask for other territories that had been conquered by Rome – she was content to rule her own hereditary lands and focused on strengthening her position. As a tribe, the Iceni were devastated by death and slavery and so, eventually, were the Brigantes, but only once Cartimandua had been forced to leave her kingdom. Both Boudica and Cartimandua were strong, capable women, often pitted against each other by the sources – they were not allies and could never have been once the Icenian queen left her pro-Roman lifestyle behind, but neither were they opposites in their moral characters.

IDENTITY

Creighton asks some pertinent questions about the effects of an exile in Rome on the British tribal royals: 'If they had been *obsides* when young, did they feel more at home in Italy or in Britain? How did they perceive themselves, as British or as Romans?' (2000, 221). Adminius and Verica would likely have had a very different experience to Cartimandua as they were male and had not ruled their people in Britain during Roman occupation. Brigantia was outside the province, was of strategic importance to Rome and as such was treated differently by the various governors and their forces. Though her actions suggest a definite political bias, Cartimandua was still a native Brigantian queen. She would have had extensive dealings with Roman officials and military men, and she may even have been to Rome to see the 'mother ship' for herself. She certainly had Roman natives in her court, but her upbringing would have profoundly affected her sense of identity. If her family had had dealings with Rome, then she may have had a gradual exposure to their culture and if she was destined to rule from birth, she would have been trained in the ways of diplomacy and government. However, although ruling their people's tribal federation, her predecessor may have been reasonably unaffected by Imperial concerns and it may have fallen to Cartimandua to carve a place for her tribe in the Empire. Whatever her early experiences, she would have known the disapproval that her status as queen caused – she may have ruled a vast kingdom and have been born into a long line of distinguished royal leaders but she would never have been totally accepted by Rome. In addition, once she embarked on the course of Roman alliance, the traditional factions of her people would have believed that she was dishonouring her roots as a native Brigantian queen.

We are used to such dilemmas in a fictional setting as they are often the subject of excellent drama. In the television productions of Bernard Cornwell's *Sharpe* series (1993-2008), the main character, Richard Sharpe, is working class and after elevation to a commission, he is torn between the privileged society of the gentleman officer and the life of a common soldier he was born to. Although Cartimandua came from much more impressive origins, both she and Sharpe tried to improve their station in life despite the disapproval of the members of both their new world and their old. The queen was surrounded by censure in both Britain and Rome – she married a Roman man, allied herself and her lands with the Empire, but still ruled her native tribe in a role she was destined to fill. The story is a common one, but usually the person struggling to better themselves is cast as the hero of the piece and not the villain. In the film *Educating Rita* (1983), the heroine is accused of only admiring the superficial elements of her new world. Having initially changed her name to Rita after a popular author she admired, she later discards it believing it to have been an affected and hollow gesture. On gaining Roman citizenship, Cartimandua may have been able to call herself Claudia Cartimandua after the emperor who bestowed the honour. Would her people have considered this change of name to be as pretentious as Rita's was? Did they see the splendour of Stanwick to be a worthless trapping of Cartimandua's new world?

Whatever the reaction to her status and gender in Rome and her chosen alliances at home, she conducted herself like a queen throughout her reign. She did not consider herself to be beneath the Roman commanders and she negotiated the terms of her support knowing the strength of her royal position. Rome may not have liked dealing with a woman but she gave them no option. If Cartimandua had been to Rome and seen their education, their baths, their aqueducts and their buildings, she may have been in awe of her surroundings at first, but it would not have taken her long to realise that they were just largely superficial advantages and that her old and new worlds were not that dissimilar. With the luxury imported goods found in her grand centre at Stanwick, Cartimandua evidently enjoyed the material benefits of Imperial influence, but this could merely show an appreciation that Roman culture was just different and not necessarily better than her own – '[its] supposed value may in the end be nothing but a prejudice' (Bramann, 2007). She worked hard to maintain the independence of the Brigantes outside the Empire and only left her tribal lands for Rome once she was forced to by her ex-husband and his rebels.

Outside of their palaces and the halls of power, were there so many differences between the average Roman and his British counterpart? Obviously, it is hard to generalise, but in many basic ways, they must have had a lot in common. Both cultures loved hunting, horses, feasting, sparring and banqueting, with the importance of family, ancestors and children to succeed them seen as central to their ways of life. The Roman and various British tribal cultures were pagan, with a wide-ranging pantheon of revered deities, and both believed in superstitions, spirits and omens in their own way. The ancient Britons believed that their soul would pass to the Otherworld, whereas in Roman law 'The Law of the Twelve Tables, first promulgated during the Republic, forbade burial within the walls of a town, so that the dead did not pollute either physically or spiritually the material world' (Alcock, 1996).

If there were any differences, they were in terms of expression. The British tribes were ostentatious with their wealth – favouring gold and brightly enamelled jewellery and accessories, painted chariots, fine cloaks and body paint, tattoos and make-up, and most of it was portable. The Romans loved to build up their homes and cities, constructing baths, forums, temples and theatres. Britons were seen as louder and less restrained, but Romans had their excesses too as the jeering mob in the arena showed. A highborn Roman and a British tribal royal may have seemed more different because their essential outlook in life – philosophy, education and what constituted moral fibre – were based on different ideals. However, the average person in each culture, removed from the prejudices of both parties (and the initial language barriers), may well have socialised at a feast or horse race quite happily. It is harder to decimate a population that is similar to your own and so the idea of the native people being hugely different from the Roman soldiers facilitated an easier conquest, especially when the invaders were convinced that the 'barbarians' could only benefit from their lands being occupied.

Cartimandua's death remains a mystery, but whether it was in Britain or in a palatial villa looking out on an Italian landscape, she was not laid to rest in the place of her ancestors. The violence of her relocation may have stopped any initial homesickness, but it must have been a strange experience for her to know that she would never see the hills of her native kingdom again. After years of conflict, infighting, rivalry and having to continually be one step ahead of her enemies to maintain calm in her realm, would Cartimandua have felt redundant in her new less visible role or would she have welcomed the opportunity to finally relax with her family? The scenario would not have been idyllic if she did settle in Rome or another part of Italy – she was a foreign barbarian queen married to a Roman native. However, she was used to the disapproval of her society and at least she would now no longer be responsible for the lives and protection of a number of people who did not agree with her methods. She would have had the dinner invitations from Roman nobles anxious to meet a 'real live barbarian queen' and after the initial novelty had worn off, she would have had the relative calm of anonymity. With time to reflect, would Cartimandua have considered the sacrifices she made to have been worth the considerable effort or would tinges of regret have cast a shadow in the brilliant Italian sunshine? After the killing and the suicides, the battles and rebellions, it would be nice if at least one barbarian queen had passed peacefully to the Otherworld, albeit in foreign waters, after a long and eventless retirement.

IMAGES AND INFLUENCE

Boudica has her statue in London, the plays, the books and no doubt some day a film, but Cartimandua has been largely relegated to a few disparaging lines in the history books. It has taken an unknown author to drag her memory from the swirling mists and hold her up to the light of modern scrutiny. Character and motivations aside, it would be wonderful if for once our own heritage could be celebrated – she was our first known queen and yet she is largely unheard of, whereas Cleopatra is a household name, if for all the wrong reasons. Elizabeth I was a great English leader and as a classically educated woman, she may even have known about Cartimandua – did she admire her ability to negotiate and make alliances with more powerful foreign powers whilst maintaining the autonomy of her kingdom, or was she swayed by the stereotypical image of a sexually immoral traitor? Elizabeth knew well the accusations of personal misconduct coming from the men who judged her as hard rather than politically shrewd and her decisions were not always popular with her court. However, both English queens had the bravery to take on those in their worlds who wished to limit them to roles that were conventionally acceptable in their own time.

Bramann (2007) describes *Educating Rita* (1983) as a film that 'celebrates leaving behind the dying of the old and the forging of a new self out of the fragments of discarded worlds.' This was what Cartimandua and all of the other ancient Britons were trying to do in making sense of their place in the new order of things after the conquest. In forensics, Locard's Principle states that every contact leaves a trace. Whether it is in the physical act of a robber smashing a window and having microscopic particles of glass transfer to their clothes, or in the intellectual act of an idea forming inspired by an earlier thought – the traces of these contacts exist even if we cannot see them or do not know they are there (Erzinclioglu, 2006, 11-12). As soon as the various British and Roman cultures in the occupied territories were exposed to each other under conditions of stress, their old worlds were contaminated – both were influenced by the other in subtle ways that increased in strength with constant reinforcement (those people living in more rural areas or away from the conquest zones had a different experience). Native art was influenced by Roman sculptures and Roman gods were merged with native deities – these examples of amalgamation would not have happened overnight though, for as both cultures shared the new experience, they also shared the inevitable initial resistance to change in some quarters. We just need to think of how our own society is bombarded with new ideas and influences in a much less stressful setting than invasion and how some of our older or more traditional members fight against this inevitable tide for as long as they can. As modern teenagers baulk at relatives who will not use the Internet or have a mobile phone, young ancient Britons, excited at the idea of going to the Roman baths, could have mocked their families for keeping their wooden bowls and refusing to eat from the new-fangled pottery dishes, or steadfastly drinking beer instead of the new types of wine. For many, these changes were born of violent beginnings, but after the battles had been fought, people had to live alongside each other.

Baudrillard (1988) said that 'it is dangerous to unmask images, since they dissimulate the fact that there is nothing behind them'. This quote could be taken very literally as it has been suggested that maybe Boudica and Cartimandua did not actually exist, but were literary creations of the ancient sources designed to make a point to their audience – an interesting idea given the amount of Roman glory that was contributed to by these women, but an unlikely one. If the 'image' was one of that person's own making, then the danger may be appreciated, but as these women cannot speak for themselves in print or otherwise (all we have are these images), they may be happy to have the propaganda and bias surrounding these narratives questioned by those who followed them. Cartimandua may certainly have encouraged such an examination if she knew the image she had been given by the sources. In challenging Tacitus' portrayal of the Brigantian queen, we enter the realms of speculation, but just because we have no alternative sources to work with, we cannot merely accept the one viewpoint we have as fact.

Stewart (1995, 1) acknowledges the problem faced when examining the testimony of these ancient writers, that of distinguishing fact from topoi (standard traditional literary themes), but believes that the sources should be appreciated in their own right as 'evidence for Roman culture and society'. Thus, Tacitus' depiction of Cartimandua may not be a factual account of the Brigantian queen, but it does tell us much about the expected attitudes to such a female figure in power in ancient Rome. The early Roman portrayal of Britain as being different, remote and unconquered beyond Ocean became a conventional image, exploited as a contrast to its own culture and manipulated to emphasise a triumph. Despite Julius Caesar's achievements in Britain and Caligula's plans for invasion, Claudius is described as the first to overcome the people on the unknown shores of Britain:

> Britain was being presented as a new horizon of conquest as if the previous century had not happened … Of course, Britain *was* known, for it was the familiarity of the image of Britain that allowed Claudius to capitalize upon its capture. The Romans had to know the British to know that they were unsubdued. But at no stage in this proclamation of power, does the 'reality' of military tactics or profit or expediency take precedence over the rhetoric of imperial expansion. Britain was a cultural symbol, and to a large extent this was the reality of Roman Britain at that time.
>
> Stewart, 1995, 9

As these persuasive techniques were applied to her country, so they were applied to her character. As a Briton and a barbarian queen, Cartimandua had two conventional images to unmask, for she was her country in Rome's eyes, both different and unconquered. Cleopatra's appearance has been changed many times over the years, with artists and writers depicting her as blond-haired and white-skinned to fit in with their ideas of beauty. However, Dio emphasised Boudica's otherness in his description of her fearsome physical appearance. Unfortunately, we do not have a similar representation of Cartimandua's looks, for however inaccurate it may have been, it would have given another aspect to her image.

It has been suggested that her name means 'sleek pony'. This could be a possible reference to the relationship between horses and kingship or a link to the spiritual significance of animals to the ancient Britons, rather than the literal description preferred by Aldhouse-Green (2006, 140): 'sleek with prosperity and sexual gratification, a beast of a woman who played out her conquests in bed rather than on the battlefield'.

Hughes-Hallett makes the excellent point that 'a single set of facts, arranged and rearranged, can point to a variety of contradictory conclusions' (2006, 12). She expands this idea in describing how everyone contributing information or presenting an argument brings with them the results of their own upbringing, needs and beliefs. In attempting to build a picture of Cartimandua, every contact leaves a trace and just as with the ancient sources, this work tells you just as much about the author as the subject being studied. A desire for objectivity is admirable but unachievable as we are all children of our time and the most we can do is acknowledge our own bias, and as with Tacitus, allow for it in forming a judgement.

We have all seen the stills in an observation test where you have to decide what was going on based on a snapshot in time. Every person asked for an opinion could give a different interpretation, but by observing the 'where', 'when' and 'who', we can examine the 'why' without assuming that we immediately know what has happened. In examining a crime scene, the investigator collects the relevant evidence and works with their forensics lab to check the veracity of a possible hunch, just as the historian relies on the archaeologist's help to support or disprove a theory based on source material. In the absence of ancient British written history, we must look at every available bit of information before we can begin to piece together any sort of feasible picture of their time.

MYTHS AND FOLKLORE

Women in antiquity were largely defined by their relationships with men – daughter, wife, mother, empress, adulteress and whore. To Rome, the former three dutiful roles depended on the male head of the household for their status, guidance, financial support and protection. The latter three were all dangerous because of their power, their independence and their exhibition of 'masculine' behaviour – the empress could have been an extension of the mother and wife category, but so many wanted much more for themselves and exploited their access to the powerful of the Empire. In the Greek and Roman pantheons, familial relationships were still imposed, so only the autonomous queen and the foreign goddess remained separate from being defined by their men and this could be why so many independent female rulers were seen as the living personification of their matron deity.

Although Cartimandua's existence is largely unacknowledged by the modern world, her portrayal as an adulteress is said to have inspired one of the most famous legends in our country, that of Arthur and Guinevere. Ziegler (1999) considers that 'the similarity between the activity of Cartimandua and the fate of Brigantia in the first century with Arthur's Queen Gwenhwyfar (Guinevere) and the fall of Arthur's realm in Geoffrey of Monmouth's *History of the Kings of Britain* is striking'. According to his version, Guanhumara/Guinevere 'violates' her first marriage to Arthur and replaces him with his trusted commander and nephew, Modred (*History of the Kings of Britain*, Book 10, Chapter 13). This was obviously meant to reflect the supposed casting aside of Cartimandua's first husband, Venutius, and the elevation of his former armour-bearer, Vellocatus. Other similarities between the two royal triangles are thought to be the employment of outside help in retaining power: Cartimandua from the Romans and Modred from the Saxons, with both stories ending in a bloody civil war and the destruction and eventual conquest of the realm by external forces. To extend the comparison, Geoffrey even set his story in what was once Brigantian territory (Collingridge, 2005, 150). However, Cartimandua certainly seems to prosper much more than her legendary counterpart, as in being rescued by her Roman allies, she begins a new life abroad, whilst Guinevere ends her days in a convent. Both women are blamed by the respective authors for the misfortunes that befall their lands, but Geoffrey's narrative is much more of a warning against the consequences of infidelity and betrayal. Vellocatus becomes royal consort in the Brigantian narrative, but in claiming Guinevere as his wife, Modred is given Arthur's lands, so if this legend and morality tale is based on Tacitus' portrayal of Cartimandua, she does not continue her role as an independent queen. Hardly a satisfactory memorial given the trouble she went through to keep her throne.

6

Conclusion

Only very slowly and late have men come to realize that unless freedom is universal it is only extended privilege.

Hill, 1961

Roman Britain was a study in the expression of freedom on a grand scale. Although many focus on the famous Boudican rebellion, there were far more instances where this concept was tested. As the above quote explains, liberty must be for all and not only for the lucky few. The rebels following Caratacus and Boudica wanted freedom from occupation, but what of the Britons who welcomed the arrival of the Roman soldiers – were they not free to explore the advantages that came from alliance with the Empire? Was freedom to choose only acceptable when the choice was a popular one? As has already been discussed, Caratacus, Boudica and Venutius only rebelled when their privileges were taken away – they were no longer free to rule as they would have wished, but their people may not have been given such liberty of choice. Members of the native tribes who did not want to go into battle were faced with the freedom to starve and stay in their lands unprotected or to leave their homes for a strange destination. The rebels were said to have championed the cause of freedom at any cost, but who was footing the bill?

Cartimandua's lands remained unoccupied by Imperial forces throughout her reign but were her people really free from the costs of invasion? The Brigantes retained their independence but gained years of internal unrest. Even after the conquest, many kingdoms were still ruled by the same monarchs on behalf of the Empire, so freedom for some may not have been greatly affected, but loyalties were definitely altered by the chain of events set in motion in AD 43. Britain was not a united kingdom but in spite of any animosity existing between the tribes, a common enemy bound a large number of the previously disunited peoples together, if only for the length of a campaign. Was this self-preservation and the comfort of safety in greater numbers or were the seeds of patriotism being sown on the battlefield? Modern thought takes for granted the notion of national pride but even that could soon be challenged.

A recent news story examined the idea that patriotism should not be taught in schools. The report from the Institute of Education in the University of London (1 February 2008) advised teaching the concept as a 'controversial issue'. Dr Michael Hand, one of the study's authors, elaborated:

> Patriotism is a love of one's country, but are countries really appropriate objects of love? Loving things can be bad for us, for example when the things we love are morally corrupt. Since all national histories are at best morally ambiguous, it's an open question whether citizens should love their countries.

The emphasis with this report is the idea of 'teaching' patriotism, but it still raises the issue of whether loving your country is controversial. National pride and freedom of expression are some of the core elements that our ancestors fought and died for, but in these days of political correctness, our speech is not quite so free. Nationality is now an insult and a man was recently given a prison sentence for calling a Welsh woman 'English' (*Daily Mail*, 30 November 2007).

Cartimandua has been accused of being unpatriotic though she did not have a country to betray and yet now that we are a united kingdom, we cannot freely express our loyalty without wondering whom we will offend. Would an ancient Briton feel right at home in modern times? We have the unpopular taxes – just like with Prasutagus, when someone dies, the government comes in and takes a big chunk of the estate – and we still have fights with the local tribe, but they are now called football derbies. In fact, sport is the only time that people do seem to be patriotic in modern times – individuals of different backgrounds, religion, colour and gender all unite under their national flag, and bond together in the face of a common enemy, just like the Boudican hordes. There has been no occupation of Britain in living memory, although my grandfather would disagree – were the Roman soldiers also thought to be 'oversexed, overpaid and over here'?

Whether she is seen as a visionary wanting more for her people or is thought to have ignored their views to pursue a path that she wanted to follow, Cartimandua will now be remembered. For in debating the pros and cons of patriotism, we can look back at the example of an ancient British queen who fought for her territory and defended her people's independence despite their rebellion against her methods. Was Cartimandua a true Brigantian patriot, for once she was overthrown, the welfare of her people suffered under the rule of those supposedly fighting for freedom?

Boudica's rebellion has had an impact in some quarters, but we still do not know enough about the people who once ruled our land. Instead of just acknowledging the Henries V and VIII and Elizabeth I, there should be more coverage of our great historical leaders. Two queens stood up to the superpower of Rome in two very different ways – one fought their soldiers on the battlefield and the other fought their prejudices, keeping her lands and her people's freedom despite the invasion of the country. Remembering our history makes us who we are, for as Cicero is thought to have said, 'To remain ignorant of things that happened before you were born is to remain a child'.

Bibliography

Alcock, J. (1996). *Life in Roman Britain.* London: Batsford

Aldhouse-Green, M. (2006). *Boudica Britannia.* Harlow: Pearson

Allason-Jones, L. (2005). *Women in Roman Britain.* London: British Museum Publications

Allen, D.F. (1963). *The Coins of the Coritani.* London: Oxford University Press

Balsdon, J.P.V.D. (1977). *Roman Women: Their History and Habits.* London: The Bodley Head Ltd

Balsdon, J.P.V.D. (1979). *Romans and Aliens.* London: Duckworth

Baudrillard, J. (1988). 'Simulacra and Simulations', *Selected Writings*, edited by Mark Poster. Cambridge: Polity Press. Available at: http://qcpages.qc.cuny.edu/ENGLISH/Staff/richter/Baudrillard.html (Accessed 28th January 2008)

Bauman, R.A. (1992). *Women and politics in ancient Rome.* London: Routledge

Berresford Ellis, P. (1990). *The Celtic Empire.* London: Constable

Berresford Ellis, P. (1998). *The Ancient World of the Celts.* New York: Barnes & Noble

Birley, A.R. (1973). 'Petillius Cerialis and the conquest of Brigantia', *Britannia* 4, 179–90

Birley, A.R. (1981). *Life in Roman Britain.* London: Batsford

Birley, E. (1976). *Roman Britain and the Roman Army.* Kendal: Titus Wilson

Bishop, M.C. (1996). *Finds from Roman Aldborough.* Oxford: Oxbow Books

Bramann, J.K. (2007). *Educating Rita and other Philosophical Movies.* Available at: http://faculty.frostburg.edu/phil/forum/EduRita.htm (Accessed 28 January 2008)

Braund, D. (1984a). *Rome and the Friendly King: The Character of the Client Kingship.* New York: St Martin's Press

Braund, D. (1984b). 'Observations on Cartimandua', *Britannia* 15, 1–6

Braund, D. (1988). 'Client Kings', in D. Braund (ed.), *The Administration of the Roman Empire (241 BC-AD 193).* University of Exeter, Department of History and Archaeology

Braund, D. (1996). *Ruling Roman Britain: Kings, Queens, Governors and Emperors from Julius Caesar to Agricola.* London: Routledge

Braund, S.H. (1992). 'Juvenal – Misogynist or Misogamist?', *The Journal of Roman Studies* 82, 71-86

Brothwell, D.R. (1986). *The Bog Man and the Archaeology of People*. London: British Museum Publications

Burn, A.R. (1969). 'Tacitus on Britain', in T. Dorey (ed.), *Tacitus*. London: Routledge and Kegan Paul

Carr, G. (2005). 'Woad, Tattooing and Identity in Later Iron Age and Early Roman Britain', *Oxford Journal of Archaeology* 24(3), 273-92

Carroll, L. (1993). *Alice in Wonderland*. Hertfordshire: Wordsworth Editions

Casson, T.E. (1945). 'Cartimandua in history, legend and romance', *Transactions of the Cumberland and Westmorland Antiquarian and Archaeological Society* 44, 68-80

Clark, A.C. (1921). '*The Reappearance of the Texts of the Classics*', paper presented to the Bibliographical Society, 21 February

Cohen, R. (2007). 'Creolization', in George Ritzer (ed.), *The Blackwell Encyclopaedia of Sociology*. Malden, MA: Blackwell

Collingridge, V. (2005). *Boudica*. London: Ebury Press

Creighton, J. (1995). 'Visions of power: imagery and symbols in late Iron Age Britain', *Britannia* 26, 285-301

Creighton, J. (2000). *Coins and Power in Late Iron Age Britain*. Cambridge: Cambridge University Press

Creighton, J. (2005). 'Gold, ritual and kingship', in Colin Haselgrove and David Wigg-Wolf (eds), *Iron Age Coinage and Ritual Practices*. Mainz Am Rhein: Verlag Philipp Von Zabern

Creighton, J. (2006). *Britannia: The creation of a Roman province*. Abingdon, Oxon: Routledge

D'Ambra, E. (2007). *Roman Women*. New York: Cambridge University Press

Davies, J. (1999). *Land of the Iceni: The Iron Age in Northern East Anglia*. Norwich: Centre of East Anglian Studies

de la Bédoyère, G. (2003). *Defying Rome: The Rebels of Roman Britain*. Stroud: Tempus

Dyson, S.L. (1975). 'Native Revolt Patterns in the Roman Empire', *ANRW: Aufstieg und Niedergang der Romischer Welt* II (3), 138-75

Ellison, R.L. (2005). *The Solitary Druid*. New York: Citadel Press Books

Erzinclioglu, Z. (2006). *Forensics*. London: Carlton Books

Fitts, R., Haselgrove, C., Lowther, P.C. & Willis, S.H. (1999). 'Melsonby reconsidered: survey and excavations 1992-5 at the site of the discovery of the "Stanwick" North Yorkshire hoard of 1843', *Durham Archaeological Journal* 14-15, 1-52

Frere, S. (1987). *Britannia*. London: Routledge and Kegan Paul

Ganor, B. (1998). 'Defining Terrorism: Is One Man's Terrorist Another Man's Freedom Fighter?', *The International Institute for Counter-terrorism*, September 23, 1998. Available at: www.ict.org.il/var/119/17070-Def%20Terrorism%20by%20Dr.%20Boaz%20Ganor.pdf (Accessed 1 January 2008)

Gibbon, E. (1845). *The History of the Decline and Fall of the Roman Empire*, notes and editing by H.H. Milman. Available at: www.sacred-texts.com/cla/gibbon/02/daf02052.htm (Accessed 22 January 2008)

Green, M. J. (2001). *Dying for the gods: human sacrifice in Iron Age & Roman Europe*. Stroud: Tempus Publishing

Hanson, W.S. (1987). *Agricola and the conquest of the North*. London: Batsford

Hanson, W.S. & Campbell, D.B. (1986). 'The Brigantes: From Clientage to Conquest', *Britannia* 17, 73-89

Hartley, B.R. & Fitts, R.L. (1988). *The Brigantes*. Gloucester: Alan Sutton Publishing

Haselgrove, C. (1989). 'Stanwick – Oppidum'. *Current Archaeology* 119, 380-5

Haselgrove, C., Turnbull, P. & Fitts, R.L. (1990). 'Stanwick, North Yorkshire, Parts 1-3', *Archaeol. J* 147, 1-90

Henig, M. (2007), 'Roman Sculpture from the Hadrian's Wall Region', *Durham University – Hadrian's Wall Research Framework*. Available at: www.dur.ac.uk/resources/archaeological.services/research_training/hadrianswall_research_framework/project_documents/Sculpture[rev].pdf (Accessed 22 January 2008)

Higham, N.J. (1986). *The Northern Counties to AD 1000*. London: Longman

Higham, N.J. (1987). 'Brigantia Revisited', *Northern History* 23, 1-19

Higham, N.J. (1993). *Rome, Britain and the Anglo-Saxons.* London: Seaby

Hill, C. (1961). *The Century of Revolution: 1603-1714*. Edinburgh: Thomas Nelson

Hind, J.G.F. (1977). 'The 'Genounian' Part of Britain', *Britannia* 8, 229-34

Hind, J.G.F. (2007). 'A. Plautius' campaign in Britain: an alternative reading of the narrative in Cassius Dio (60.19.5-21.2)', *Britannia* 38, 93-106

Hingley, R. & Unwin, C. (2005). *Boudica: Iron Age Warrior Queen*. London: Hambledon

Hoffmann, S. (1968). 'Collaborationism in France during World War II', *Journal of Modern History* 40 (3), 375-95

Holland, R. (2000). *Nero: The man behind the myth*. Stroud: Sutton Publishing

Hughes-Hallett, L. (2006). *Cleopatra: queen, lover, legend*. London: Pimlico

Hyde, D. (1901). *A Literary History of Ireland From Earliest Times to the Present Day*. New York: Scribner

Jackson, R.L. (2000). 'The Sense and Sensibility of Betrayal: Discovering the Meaning of Treachery through Jane Austen'. *Humanitas* XIII, 2, 72-89. Available at: www.nhinet.org/jackson13-2.pdf (Accessed 30 December 2007)

James, S. (1999). *The Atlantic Celts: Ancient people or modern invention?* London: British Museum Press

James, S. (2001). 'The Roman Galley Slave: *Ben-Hur* and the Birth of a Factoid', *Public Archaeology* 2 (1), 35-49

Jones, T. and Ereira, A. (2006). *Terry Jones' Barbarians: An Alternative Roman History*. Reading: Random House

MacKillop, J. (2006). *Myths and Legends of the Celts.* London: Penguin

Mattingly, D. (2006). *An Imperial Possession: Britain in the Roman Empire.* London: Allen Lane

McNeill, T. (1998). *La collaboration d'etat or State Collaboration.* Available at: http://seacoast.sunderland.ac.uk/~os0tmc/occupied/collab.htm (Accessed 28 January 2008)

Mitchell, S. (1978). 'Venutius and Cartimandua', *Liverpool Classical Monthly* iii, 215-9

Morgan, V. & Morgan, P. (2004). *Prehistoric Cheshire.* Ashbourne, Derbyshire: Landmark Publishing Company

Netanyahu, B. (1985). *Terrorism: How The West Can Win.* New York: Farrar, Strauss and Giroux

Pomeroy, S.B. (1975). *Goddesses, whores, wives and slaves: women in classical antiquity.* New York: Schocken Books

Pryor, F. (2004). *Britain bc.* London: HarperCollins

Ramm, H. (1980). 'Native Settlements East of the Pennines', in Keith Branigan (ed.), *Rome and the Brigantes: The Impact of Rome on Northern England.* Sheffield: University of Sheffield, Dept of Prehistory and Archaeology

Reed, N. (1977). *Studien zu den Militärgrenzen Roms 2: Vorträge des 10. Internationalen Limeskongresses in der Germania Inferior* (10th International Congress of Roman Frontier Studies), 41-3. Koln: Rheinland-Verlag

Richmond, I.A. (1944). 'Gnaevs Ivlivs Agricola', *The Journal of Roman Studies* 34, 34-45

Richmond, I.A. (1954). 'Queen Cartimandua', *Journal of Roman Studies* xliv, 43-52

Ross, A. (1961). 'The Horned God of the Brigantes', *Archaeologia Aeliana* 4 (39), 63-86

Ross, A. (1999). *Druids.* Stroud: Tempus

Ross, A. & Robins, D. (1989). *The Life and Death of a Druid Prince: The story of an archaeological sensation.* London: Rider

Salway, P. (1981). *Roman Britain.* Oxford: Oxford University Press

Sealey, P.R. (2004). *The Boudican Revolt against Rome.* Buckinghamshire: Shire Archaeology

Singh, G. (1972). 'The Truth about the Indian Mutiny of 1857', *The Sikh Review*, August 1972. Available at: www.sikhspectrum.com/082004/1857_mutiny_g_s.htm (Accessed 21 January 2008)

Snook, M. (2008). 'The myth of native-bashing', *BBC History Magazine* 9(1), 31-3

Stead, I.M., Bourke, J.B. & Brothwell, D. (1986). *Lindow Man – the Body in the Bog.* London: British Museum Publications

Stewart, P.C.N. (1995). 'Inventing Britain: The Roman Creation and Adaptation of an Image', *Britannia* 26, 1-10

Stone, M. (1976). *When God was a woman.* Florida: Harcourt Brace & Company

Townend, G. (1961). 'Some Flavian Connections', *The Journal of Roman Studies* 51 (1-2)

Trow, M.J. (2003). *Boudicca*. Stroud: Sutton Publishing

Turnbull, W.B. (ed.) (1858). *The Buik of the Croniclis of Scotland, or, A Metrical Version of the History of Hector Boece by William Stewart*. London: Longman, Brown, Green, Longmans and Roberts

Turnbull, P. & Fitts, L. (1988). 'The Politics of Brigantia', in J. Price & P.R. Wilson (eds), *Recent Research in Roman Yorkshire*. BAR British Series 193, 377-86

Turner, R.C. and Scaife, R.G. (eds) (1995). *Bog Bodies: New Discoveries and New Perspectives*. London: British Museum Press

Waite, J. (2007). *Boudica's Last Stand: Britain's Revolt Against Rome AD 60-61*. Stroud: Tempus

Webster, G. (1993a). *Rome Against Caratacus: The Roman Campaigns in Britain AD 48-58*. London: B.T. Batsford

Webster, G. (1993b). *Boudica: The British Revolt Against Rome AD 60*. London: B.T. Batsford

Webster, J. (1999). 'At the End of the World: Druidic and Other Revitalization Movements in Post-Conquest Gaul and Britain', *Britannia* 30: 1-20

Webster, J. (2001), 'Creolizing the Roman Provinces', *American Journal of Archaeology* 105, 209-25

Wellesley, K. (1954). 'Can you trust Tacitus?', *Greece and Rome* 1(1), 13-33

Wellesley, K. (1969). 'Tacitus as a Military Historian', in T. Dorey (ed.), *Tacitus*. London: Routledge and Kegan Paul

Wheeler, M. (1954). *The Stanwick fortifications, North Riding of Yorkshire*. Oxford University Press for the Society of Antiquaries

Williams, J. (2005). ''The newer rite is here': vinous symbolism on British Iron Age coins', in C. Haselgrove & D. Wigg-Wolf (eds), *Iron Age Coinage and Ritual Practices*. Mainz Am Rhein: Verlag Philipp Von Zabern

Wilson, D.R. & Wright, R.P. (1965). 'Roman Britain in 1964: I. Sites Explored: II. Inscriptions', *The Journal of Roman Studies* 55 (1-2), 199-228

Wolfson, S. (2002). *Tacitus, Thule and Caledonia: A critical reinterpretation of the textual problems*. Available at: http://myweb.tiscali.co.uk/fartherlands/ (Accessed 22 January 2008)

Woodman, T. (1979). 'Self imitation and the substance of history: Tacitus, Annals 1.61-5 and Histories 2.70, 5.14-15', in D. West & T. Woodman (eds), *Creative imitation and Latin Literature*. Cambridge: Cambridge University Press

Ziegler, M. (1999). 'Brigantia, Cartimandua and Gwenhwyfar', *The Heroic Age*, Issue 1, Spring/Summer 1999. Available at: www.mun.ca/mst/heroicage/issues/1/habcg.htm (Accessed 1 June 2007)

INTERNET REFERENCES

WordNet 1.7.1. Princeton University, 2001. '*insurgent, insurrectionist, freedom fighter, rebel.*' Available at: www.answers.com/topic/insurgent-insurrectionist-freedom-fighter-rebel (Accessed 1 January 2008)

The British Museum, '*Victim of a sacrifice?*' Available at: www.britishmuseum.org/explore/highlights/highlight_objects/pe_prb/l/lindow_man.aspx (Accessed 4 January 2008)

University of Notre Dame Latin Dictionary. Available at: www.nd.edu/~archives/latin.htm (Accessed 17th January 2008)

Institute of Education, University of London, '*Patriotism too controversial to promote in schools*'. Available at: http://ioewebserver.ioe.ac.uk/ioe/cms/get.asp?cid=1397&1397_1=18020 (Accessed 1 February 2008)

Index

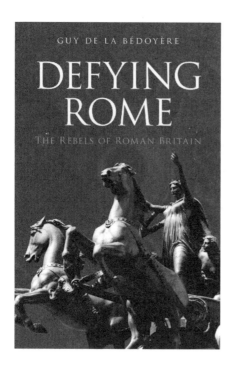

**Defying Rome –
The Rebels of Roman Britain**

Guy de la Bédoyère

£17.99
Paperback
978 0 7524 4440 6
224pp (+16 colour pages)

The power of the Roman Empire was under constant challenge. Nowhere was this truer than in Britain, Rome's remotest and most recalcitrant province.

A succession of idealists, chancers and reactionaries fomented dissent and rebellion. Some, like Caratacus and Boudica, were tribal chiefs wanting to expel Rome and recover lost power. Others were military opportunists such as Carausius and Allectus, who wanted to become emperor and were prepared to exploit everything Britain had to offer to support their bids for power.

Each of these rebellions reads like a story in itself, combining archaeology with the dramatic testimony of the historical and epigraphic sources, and explains why Britain was such a hot-bed of dissent.

www.thehistorypress.co.uk